The Dil...

R(...

TE...

EBENEEZER DIBBLEE (m. Mary Wakefield)

WAKEFIELD DIBBLEE (m. Jane Fyler)

EBENEEZER DIBBLEE

EBENEEZER DIBBLEE Jr. (m. Mary Hardy)

FYLER DIBBLEE (m. Frances Wilson)

ALBERT DIBBLEE (m. Annie Meecham)	**THOMAS** (m. Francisca de la Guerra)	NELLIE	WILLIAM	HENRY
BENJAMIN — ANITA — ALBERT — HARRISON				

TERESA	FRANCISCA (m. Wm. T. Summers)	YNEZ*	**MERCEDES** (m. Alfred R. Poett)	WILSON (m. Anita Oreña)	CARMELITA (m. Francis T. Underhill)	WILLIAM	DELFINA
DIBBLEE	FRANCES			THOMAS	VIRGINIA	YVONNE	RICHARD

FREDERICA	YNEZ NANICE MERCEDES (m. C.E. Russell)	**ALFRED DIBBLEE**	HAROLD HOWARD (m. Mary Louise Hart)

The Poett Family

DR. JOSEPH HENRY POETT (m. Sarah Susanna Wood)

AGNES (m. Wm. D.M. Howard)	**ALFRED** (m. Mary Louise Williams)	JULIA (m. John Redington)
GEORGE (m. George Howard)		

HENRY	GERTRUDE	THEODORE (m. Oliva Lansdale)	ALFRED	JULIA	ARTHUR	SARAH	JOHN	LAWRENCE (m. Josephine Parrott)

HENRY W. (m. Genevieve Garolan)	MARION (m. Henry Howard)	**ALFRED R.** (m. Mercedes Dibblee)	MABEL (m. Carl Francis Edwards)

FREDERICA	YNEZ NANICE MERCEDES (m. C.E. Russell)	**ALFRED DIBBLEE**	HAROLD HOWARD (m. Mary Louise Hart)

Regards to the See family of Refugio

A. Dibblee Poett

Casa San Julian

Rancho San Julian

The story of a California ranch and its people

A. DIBBLEE POETT

A JIM COOK EDITION
Fithian Press · Santa Barbara Historical Society
SANTA BARBARA · 1991

Design and typography by Jim Cook

Co-published by Fithian Press, Post Office Box 1525, Santa Barbara, California 93102, and the Santa Barbara Historical Society, 136 East De la Guerra Street, Santa Barbara, California 93101.

LIBRARY OF CONGRESS CATALOGING-IN-PUBLICATION DATA
Poett, A. Dibblee, 1906-
    Rancho San Julian: the history of a Santa Barbara rancho /
A. Dibblee Poett
      p.   c.m.
    "A Jim Cook edition"
    Includes bibliographical references.
    ISBN 0-931832-71-3
    1. Rancho San Julian (Calif.)—History.   2. Ranch life—
California—Santa Barbara County—History.   3. Santa Barbara
County (Calif.)—History.   1. Title.
F869.R1965P64   1990
979.4'91—dc20   90-45332
                                                               CIP

Contents

Dedication xiii

Preface (by James Poett) xv

Foreword xix

Introduction: A Ride to Purísima xxi

I. A History

Location and Topography 3

The de la Guerras 8

The Sons and Daughters of José de la Guerra 39

Dibblees and Hollisters 45

The Land Act of 1851 71

Henry Dibblee .77

The Poetts 81

Efforts to Buy and Sell San Julian 87

II. Into the Twentieth Century

Rancho San Julian 93

Casa San Julian .97

The San Julian Road 103

Fencing 110

The Wharf at Gaviota 115

The Gas Pipeline 119

III. Life on the Ranch

The Men of San Julian 125
Sheepherding 136
Cattle Ranching 145
Oil and Geology and Tom Dibblee 160
Diatomaceous Earth 166
Richard Bond 171
Tramps 175

IV. Recollections 177

Appendix

The Last Will and Testament of Juan Guiterre Guerra 225
Bibliography and Notes 229

List of Illustrations

Cattle drive on Rancho San Julian (ca. 1935) . . . . *cover*
  Photograph by Hobart O. Skofield; hand tinting by Eileen Avolio; courtesy
  of Frederica Dibblee Poett

Three views of the ranch . . . . *back cover*
  Photographs by William B. Dewey, 1990

A. Dibblee Poett and Musica . . . . *back flap*
  Photograph by Bruce Weber, 1986

Casa San Julian . . . . *frontispiece*
  Photograph by William B. Dewey, 1990

Lt. John Richard Francis Dibblee xiii
  Courtesy of Thomas W. Dibblee, Jr.

Lt. James Robert Oreña Rickard xiii
  Photograph by Lansing Brown; courtesy of John T. Rickard

San Julian Valley, ca. 1875 4
  Photograph by E.J. Hayward; courtesy of Clifton F. Smith

San Julian Valley, 1990 5
  Photograph by William B. Dewey

Pacífico Ortega House, ca. 1900 7
  Courtesy of Frederica Dibblee Poett

Noriega family coat of arms 9

Torre Noriega 14
  Courtesy of Frederica Dibblee Poett

Torre de la Guerra 15
  Courtesy of Frederica Dibblee Poett

Escutcheon at Torre de la Guerra 16
  Photograph by A. Dibblee Poett, 1972

De la Guerra family coat of arms 17

Casa de la Guerra, ca. 1900 24
    Photograph by N.H. Reed; courtesy of Frederica Dibblee Poett

Capitán José de la Guerra 25
    Painting by Leonardo Barbieri, 1856; courtesy of Santa Barbara Historical
    Society

Indian rebellion of 1824 29
    Drawing by Alexander F. Harmer; from Engelhardt, *Santa Barbara Mission*
    (San Francisco, 1923)

Diseño for Rancho San Julian 35
    Courtesy of Santa Barbara Historical Society

Pablo Andrés de la Guerra 40
    Courtesy of Santa Barbara Historical Society

Josefa Moreno y Castro de la Guerra 41
    Courtesy of Santa Barbara Historical Society

Miguel de la Guerra and Captain Antonio de la Guerra 42
    Courtesy of Santa Barbara Historical Society

Sala of Casa de la Guerra, 1876 43
    Photograph by E.J. Hayward; courtesy of Frederica Dibblee Poett

Ana Maria de la Guerra Robinson .44
    Courtesy of Frederica Dibblee Poett

William Welles Hollister and Joseph Cooper 50
    From Sands, *A Pastoral Prince* (Santa Barbara, 1893)

Thomas Bloodgood Dibblee 62
    Photograph by N.H. Reed, ca. 1890

Francisca de la Guerra Dibblee 62
    Courtesy of Santa Barbara Historical Society

Beach at Santa Barbara and Punta del Castillo, ca. 1887 63
    Photographs by I.N. Cook; courtesy of Santa Barbara Historical Society

Judge Ogden Hoffman 70
    From Hoffman, *Hoffman's Land Cases* (San Francisco, 1862)

Henry Dibblee 79
    Courtesy of Frederica Dibblee Poett

Alfred Poett and Mary Louise Williams Poett 83
    Courtesy of Santa Barbara Historical Society

Alfred Redington Poett 84
Courtesy of Frederica Dibblee Poett

Surveying bill from Alfred Poett 85

T. Wilson Dibblee 89

Views of Casa San Julian 98-101
Photographs by William B. Dewey, 1990

San Julian Ranch headquarters 102
Photograph by Wiliam B. Dewey, 1990

Cave at Las Cuevitas 107
Photograph by Robert Craig

Cattle brands 113

Gaviota, ca. 1875 116
Courtesy of Dr. Charles E. Piper

Alfredo Espinosa 126

Caterpillar tractor 132

Bean harvesting, ca. 1915 133

C.E. Russell 134

Sheep at San Julian 137

Sheep shearing token 140

Alfredo Espinosa and his sheep 142

Rancho San Julian School, ca. 1912 143

Cattle drive at El Jaro, ca. 1935 146
Photograph by Frederica Dibblee Poett

Roundup in Los Amoles Valley, ca. 1940 147
Photograph by Preston Duncan

Roundup in the Ytias, ca. 1950 149

Handling a steer 150
Photograph by Wilkes, ca. 1940

Cattle branding, ca. 1940 151
Photograph by Preston Duncan

Cattle dipping, ca. 1910 155

Thomas W. Dibblee, Jr. 161

Geologic map of San Julian 162
    Drawn by Thomas W. Dibblee, Jr.

Yvonne Dibblee Donohoe 164
    Courtesy of Santa Barbara Historical Society

Virginia Dibblee 164
    Photograph by Wilkes, ca. 1940; courtesy of Santa Barbara Historical
    Society

Diatomaceous earth mine from the air 167
    Photograph by William B. Dewey, 1990

Diatomaceous earth mine 168
    Photograph by William B. Dewey, 1990

Lake on Los Palos Colorados 169

Calf among sycamores 173
    Photograph by A. Dibblee Poett, ca. 1947

Kitchen entrance, Casa San Julian 176
    Photograph by Donald Murchie, 1969

Frederica, Nan, and Dibblee Poett, ca. 1915 180
    Courtesy of Santa Barbara Historical Society

Augustín Rios with reata 183

Frances Summers and Dibblee Summers 185

Mercedes Dibblee Poett and friends 194
    Courtesy of Frederica Dibblee Poett

Frederica and Harold Poett, 1921 196
    Courtesy of Santa Barbara Historical Society

Frederica Dibblee Poett 197
    Painting by Cecil Clark Davis, ca. 1935

Harold Poett, 1946 198

Poett house in Santa Barbara 203
    Photograph by G.H.S. Harding; courtesy of Delfina Russell Mott

Family gathering, 1918 205
    Courtesy of Frederica Dibblee Poett

T. Wilson Dibblee and Ynez Dibblee, 1924 206
    Photograph by Bouchard

Family during Fiesta, 1924 208
    Photograph by Bouchard; courtesy of Clifton Smith

Ynez Dibblee 211

James Poett 212
    Courtesy of Harold H. Poett

William and Susan Poett 212

Joseph Russell 213
    Photograph by Antonia de la Guerra

Caroline Russell 213
    Painting by Douglas E. Parshall

Delfina Russell Mott 213
    Drawing by Douglas E. Parshall

Anita Oreña Dibblee and grandchildren 214
    Photograph by Karl Obert, ca. 1950

Juan Toto, ca. 1910 220

MAPS

CARTOGRAPHY BY DAVID F. MYRICK

Southwestern Santa Barbara County Ranches 2

Map of the Rancho San Julian 92

Lt. John Richard Francis Dibblee

Lt. James Robert Oreña Rickard

THIS BOOK IS DEDICATED to the memory of two worthy descendants of José de la Guerra who gave their lives for their country in World War II.

ROBERT RICKARD was the eldest child of James B. and Acacia Oreña Rickard of Santa Barbara. A more fun-loving and jolly fellow it would be hard to find. Robert spent much of his time at the family ranch, called Cuyama, which had been granted to his grandmother, María Antonia Lataillade, a daughter of José de la Guerra. Robert spent time in Santa Barbara and Los Angeles, where he was acquainted with many of the movie celebrities. He joined the U.S. Navy after the outbreak of war and was a lieutenant on the aircraft carrier U.S.S. *Franklin*. The carrier was engaged in a battle in the Sea of Japan and was badly hit and on fire; many of the crew were ordered overboard. Robert was severely injured so that when he finally got into the water he was unable to keep afloat, despite the heroic efforts of his shipmates. He expired there.

RICHARD DIBBLEE was the youngest child of Wilson and Anita Oreña Dibblee of Santa Barbara. He joined the Army Air Corps shortly after the outbreak of World War II. He became a lieutenant and was assigned to a B-25 bomber stationed in the Pacific. During a bombing run from Guam, his plane was hit and went down at sea with the loss of all its crew. The loss of Richard Dibblee was a cruel blow to his loving parents and siblings; his memory as a fine, upright young man will remain with us always.

Harold Poett, my brother, and Jack Rickard, my cousin, also deserve recognition for their contribution toward defeat of the enemy in the Great War.

Harold was an infantryman who fought all through the campaign in Italy, starting with the terrible Anzio battle and through the defeat of the Germans in Italy. He came home unscathed.

John Rickard joined the Navy and, as lieutenant and gunnery officer on a destroyer, saw action in the Pacific. He returned without wounds. He started his own law practice and, after several years, served two terms as mayor of Santa Barbara. He afterward returned to his law offices, only to serve fifteen years as Santa Barbara County Superior Court judge. None of his decisions was ever overturned on appeal.

PREFACE

WHEN MY WIFE and daughter and I moved to Rancho San Julian in 1980 to raise cattle, my uncle, Dibblee Poett, gave me his 1937 edition of Morrison's *Feed and Feeding*, suggesting that if I was going to be in this business I had to understand its basic principles, a few of which he believed had gotten obscured in the intervening years.

It is hard to recognize the effect World War II had on agriculture without going back to 1936. Published just around the time of the invention of the moveable hay baler, the tractor could still be considered an expensive supplement to the horse and mule. A photograph in the book, captioned "efficient machinery," showed hay being loaded onto horse-drawn wagons and two men with pitch forks. It was not that Dibbs did not keep current with modern commercial agriculture. He just didn't approve of the excesses and artificial dependencies to which post-World War II farmers have become addicted. With time and experience I came to appreciate the wisdom of this point of view

Feed and Feeding was at first more helpful in identifying a Fresno scraper rusting beside a shed than helping me become conservent with modern methods. The nutrition tables were much the same, but I trusted modern books more. As years passed, however, the occasional details began to take on a credibility and practicality that surpassed most contemporary textbooks. Written in the same kind of nuts-and-bolts style as the Caterpillar maintenance manuals of the 1950's, *Feed and Feeding* asked questions like: When was the best time of day to cut hay? It was the answer to this kind of question that Dibblee would feel obliged to pin to my gate.

Dibbs and I live within shouting distance of each other, but he likes to put things down on paper. And usually, as far as I was concerned, on the back of old envelopes. I kept a file of these notes, which were succinct and dealt with a particular problem that needed correction.

When, after a rain, some cows slipped through a break in a fence and got into my oat fields, I found pinned to my gate a pencil outline of a hoof print with the words "12 sq in" within the drawing. Stapled to the back was a handwritten explanation of compaction, the weight of a cow, a discussion of soil mechanics, and how, even in the Lompoc Valley, fertility is being diminished by the use of wheel tractors instead of crawlers.

About five years ago, I received a formal note from Dibbs typed on a piece of unused stationery, in a matching envelope with the flap tucked under. It was time to sell my calf crop, and I had the option of sending them through the local auction, as I usually did, or selling them directly to a buyer from Visalia. When I decided, as did a number of neighbors, that the buyer would give a better price than the sales yard, it meant that the cattle must be weighed and paid for on the ranch. Dibbs's note, which I received the evening before the buyer was scheduled to arrive, gave me rather explicit instructions on how I was to handle the deal. The most important thing, Dibbs wrote, is that I must take charge of the weighing and not let the buyer manipulate the scales. Dibbs's instructions were minute and focused entirely on the scale's "beam." I should not allow the buyer to get to the beam first. "It is a psychological thing that would allow a buyer to dominate a position." Wilson, Dibbs's uncle who had run the San Julian through much of the first half of this century, had always taken charge of the scale. There were too few advantages in the hands of the seller in this business to allow for waste.

Our spoken conversations—at least about the land—have also developed a remarkable shorthand of their own. The last truly unabbreviated communication was back in the spring of 1974 in the ranch office. I was on the ranch helping to reroof the wool barn. The sheep were long gone, but we kept old equipment in the barn. It was evening. The light in the office is a seventy-five-watt bulb within a faded manila shade over a single-drawered, white kitchen table covered with green oil cloth and a blue blotter. Book shelves built out from the adobe wall house the volumes of the Shorthorn Herd Book, from volume one (1873 ed.) through the Second World War. The older volumes were pushed back behind the newer so that they lay two deep on the shelves. The books from the Depression and war sit on top. Some photographs of the Clydesdales that powered the ranch before diesel are taped to the adobe wall near a framed picture of prize-winning sides of beef at the California State Fair. The old 1893 map of the San Julian, drawn by Dibbs's father's father for his mother's father has been on the wall behind the desk for as long as anyone can remember. The conversation had to do with ownership of land and the contingent rights and privileges.

Dibbs's views on the subject were—and remain—remarkably similar to his concept of machinery. A good Wisconsin engine purchased just back in the thirties, if it's been kept up and under cover when not in use, still has a lot of good use left. Equipment is a factor of original quality and the care that is put into it. This idea is only magnified when applied to the land. The history of a piece of land is the history of the care taken of it. The land should be in better shape when he turns over the reins to management than when the manager first took over. Dibbs will badger me into a serious conversation about amortizing a fence over one hundred years, but the land must last forever. That is what agriculture is about.

Our conversations have trimmed down considerably over the years. Two years ago, Dibbs stopped me on the road. We were just into spring and already there was summer dust in the air. It was still early in what was to become one of the worst droughts of the century. We had been driving past each other on the dirt road. He raised his hand—he wanted to speak to me. Dibbs got out of his car and started walking into the field so I got out of my truck and followed. He grabbed a fist full of grass and came back to where I stood. His hands are thick and gnarled like oak. He held out the clump of green young rye and oats just coming into head.

"Why does the grass grow?" he demanded.

I told him it grew to seed itself. He nodded and waited.

What he wanted from me was the number and time I would begin taking cattle off the grassland. Up until this moment he had been sanguine about another rain. For the last month he had been telling anyone who asked that the year wouldn't end on a frost, meaning that after the last frost of the winter there would still be one more good rain. Cattle *are* grassland. They are sustained by it and they perpetuate it. But the definition of how much the cattle take and how the rancher saves varies, as in every other business, in the eye of the beholder—especially in a bad year.

Dibbs has a notoriously cold eye. For years he had been talking about those "devil winds" from the south that J.W. Cooper wrote about in his letters in 1863 (the beginning years of the great drought of that century). The north wind had come up several days before and he'd told me plenty that an unyielding spring north wind was a drought.

"You know the year never ends on a frost," I told him. He looked me over. "It's only March, Dibbs."

"You've got 'til April first to let me know," he said. He dropped the grass and got back into his car.

"You better start praying," he said, and drove off.

Whether through my prayers or a more general fate, we did in fact get another rain that year. Not enough to diminish the drought, but enough to bring along the grass.

Family gossip about the San Julian always claimed the ranch's real value was seen best in bad years. In the drought during the Civil War the San Julian was one of the only ranches in the state to bring up feed. These kinds of oral traditions about a plot of land are the stuff of agriculture. Dibbs understands this. He has taken down these traditions and researched the facts and put them in this book. He also spent a great deal of time and research in the more general history of California. It was time well spent. Dibbs is not a man who wavers much when he sets his mind on something, and he set his mind on the San Julian a good number of years ago. I know that I and the rest of the family are grateful that he did, because what the San Julian is now and what it means largely comes from him.

JAMES POETT

Rancho San Julian
Summer 1990

xviii

FOREWORD

IN WRITING the story of Rancho San Julian, it was deemed appropriate that the histories of the de la Guerra, Dibblee, Hollister, and Cooper families should be included. No attempt has been made to write an historical novel. Dialogue has been kept to a minimum, since most communication between the participants was in writing, from letters and other accounts of their lives. I have attempted to make this work as historically accurate as possible. The story of the four families spans virutally all of the nineteenth century. This history of twentieth-century Rancho San Julian is, of course, not entirely objective, as it is seen through my eyes, but it covers most of the important events of this century for about eighty years.

I wish to acknowledge the assistance of the following people who helped me in my endeavor. First of all is the late Selden Spaulding of Santa Barbara, who persuaded me to write this story. The efforts of Señorita Maria del Carmen Tapia of Santa Barbara and Madrid revealed the valuable documents from the Archivos de Santander in Spain.

I wish to thank Bill Richardson, who directed my writing; Harold and Diana Ormsby, Jane Yokoyama, and Jennie Larvick, who assisted me with the translations of many documents from the de la Guerra archives in the Santa Barbara Mission; the late Reverend Maynard Geiger, who assisted in the search of those well-catalogued archives; Dr. James Hart of the Bancroft Library at the University of California at Berkeley, who assisted me in and directed me to the Dibblee letters there, and who gave me permission to publish from those letters. James J. Hollister III loaned me the story of Hollister's sheep drive and his activities in California, written by the late Walker Tompkins, without which this story would have never been completed. Chris Lauer unearthed the *Congressional Globe* at the University of California at Santa Barbara and found there the unpublished manuscripts of Rose Avina and Adele Ogden, both of which have given an historical perspective. I owe a debt to the late Reverend Joseph Thompson, a distant cousin, whose comprehensive study of the life of José de la Guerra he published after thorough research.

To all who have assisted and furnished constructive criticism in my long attempt to complete this work, I give thanks to: Audrey Berman for transcribing the manuscript; Marianne Partridge for assistance and encouragement; James Poett for his preface; David Myrick of the Santa Barbara Historical Society for his editing and help in mapping; John Woodward for help with editing the illustrations; and Jim Cook, for the design and final editing of my rambling manuscript.

With this perspective, beginning with the arrival in California of José de la Guerra in 1801 until the deaths of Albert and Thomas Dibblee in 1895, nearly the whole of the nineteenth century lay before me—with its earthquakes, fires, floods, droughts, political and economic upheavals, the Gold Rush, and changes in the ecology, agriculture, and the pastoral way of California life. While my subject is but a microcosm of these broader events, it was unalterably shaped by them.

The ranch remains an island out of the past. An anachronism, if you will, it resists the change to urbanization that plagues so much of our beautiful state. It clings to that past, attempting to survive while the twentieth century whizzes by with its missiles roaring up over the nearby hills of Vandenberg Air Force Base and traffic zooming past the entrance gate to Casa San Julian.

A Ride to Purísima

EARLY one spring morning in 1816, a small troop of Spanish cavalry left Mission Santa Inés bound for Mission La Purísima Nueva in the Lompoc Valley, led by the newly installed comandante of the Santa Barbara presidio, Capitán Don José Antonio Julian de la Guerra y Noriega. The contingent comprised a subaltern, seven enlisted men, and an Indian from the mission at Santa Barbara. The Indian had been included at the behest of de la Guerra, who wished to learn more about the trees and herbs of the region.

On the way over San Marcos Pass, the Indian had pointed out to de la Guerra a heavy stand of chapparal that contained several different species of plants. The name chaparral applied to the general brush of the mountainside, which the Indians burned off every few years so that the deer could graze on the new growth. Among the plants of the chaparral were ceaenothus, buckthorn, chamiso (*sp. baccharis*), and a few other bushy species such as *hierba del oso* (bear berry), sometimes called *cascara sagrada* (bitter bark), which the Indians used as an astringent and cathartic. The bears and raccoons and possums and even the birds fed on the berries of this bush, which attains a height of ten to fifteen feet. Under this mass of growth was found the *hierba buena*, with which the *capitan* was familiar, as it grew well all along the California coast.

Shortly before reaching Mission Santa Inés, the Indian pointed out an herb in the Sanja Cota Creek called *hierba mansa*, which the Indians eagerly sought on account of its scarcity and reputed medicinal properties.

Instead of proceeding down the Valley of La Purísima, as it was called, the group crossed the river near the mission and rode southward through Rancho Nojoqui, where they encountered the magnificent stand of *alisos* (sycamores), for which the valley is named. They were shown the laurel, or bay trees, that the Indians used against headaches, and the stand of huge *robles* and *encinos* (white oaks and canyon live oaks), both of which supplied the Indians with food.

They continued up what is now called the Nojoqui grade and descended the other side to a point where they encountered two canyons bearing in from the northwest. They rode up the second one, which we know today as Las Nutrias, to the west.

After a mile or so, they veered to the left to mount a steep hill, now called Las Cruces Grade, and at the summit they stopped to rest their horses and take in the magnificent view ahead of them. In the distance they could see Tranquillon Mountain and the hills of La Tinta, where the tan-bark oak approaches its last stand before the sea, about two miles to the east—where the San Julian, Jalama, and Hollister ranches now meet. Wisps of fog drifted over the distant hills, indicating a westerly breeze that soon cooled their horses.

They proceeded down the lesser incline to the west, approaching the flatlands where the creeks of Los Llanitos and Yridises joined near an Indian encampment. Willows, box elders, and the stately *álamo* lined the creek, where *berros* (watercress) grew in the flowing stream. The elderberry, whose fruit the Indians awaited with anticipation, were just in bloom.

On across the flatlands of La Golondrina and El Álamo, with its heavy, black *agueda* adobe, and over the hills of El Atascoso they rode, gazing with wonder at the rugged mountains that intrude the valley to the south. The huge forests of live oak in the canyons and hills of Los Yridises and Los Llanitos were visible, as were the gently rolling and sloping hills of El Álamo. The creek continued near the surface, winding around the foothills of El Atascoso to where it emerged from the narrow canyon we now call La Cadena to reveal a large flatlands where the mountain chain veers off to the south.

There the alluvial plain was about a mile wide across the valley and nearly two miles long, with three canyons whose streams carried water out of the Santa Rosa Hills, to the north.

Near the middle of the three streams and nestled against the foothills on the north side of the valley they were surprised to find a small adobe hut. One of the soldiers said it had been constructed by a priest and a soldier who used to go that way to Mission La Purísima instead of making their way up the coast past Point Concepción and over the hills into Miguelito Canyon. That structure, legend has it, was constructed around 1805 on the site of the present Casa San Julian. The foundations of that early building were found under the present house, attesting to the truth of the legend.

The soldiers had brought some *carne seca* (jerky) and some bread and wine, which they partook at the site of the cabin, and de la Guerra lingered there until reminded that they had fifteen miles further to go to reach Mission La Purísima. They rode the rest of the valley, which opened up a short way past Los Palos Colorados, onto the large flats of Salsipuedes ("get out if you can"). The flats gave them a view of the northern side of Rancho Jalama, which was to become a part of the San Julian land grant.

The party reached Mission La Purísima just before dark and were warmly welcomed by the padres there. The padres were struggling to complete a new structure to replace the older mission, which had been built near an earthquake fault and had fallen in the quake of 1812. The new mission was being built nearly a mile and a half away, about as far across the upper end of the valley as possible.

The above is my fantasized account of how José de la Guerra first saw San Julian. However it occurred, see it he did, and in 1816 he was able to persuade the governor, Don Pablo Vincente de Solá, to declare a tract of land comprising about eleven and a half square leagues (about 48,000 acres) as a royal rancho to serve the Presidio of Santa Barbara with horses and cattle.

When Mexico gained its independence from Spain in 1821 after a struggle of about eleven years, the ranch was renamed Rancho Nacional San Julian. The titles of nearly all of the *repartimiento* (provisional grants made by the Spanish government) were invalidated, although several of those were later regranted by the Mexican government to the original grantees. In 1837, after his seizure of power from Governor Gutiérrez in 1836, Governor Alvarado granted the rancho to Don José de la Guerra, who was still comandante of the presidio at Santa Barbara.

Later, financially weakened by the long struggle to prove their title to San Julian and threatened with bankruptcy by the disastrous drought of 1862-64, the de la Guerras were forced to mortgage their ranch to a man named Gaspar Oreña. Oreña sold the land to the Dibblee-Hollister partnership in 1867. Shortly thereafter, Thomas Dibblee married Francisca de la Guerra, the granddaughter of the original owner.

Succeeding generations have lived on Rancho San Julian and have formed a strong attachment to the land. Despite great depressions, world wars, droughts, and some forced sales, together with the need for a higher return on the land, they have made strenuous efforts to keep the ranch intact. On the whole, harmony has prevailed among the owners, whose incomes have been enhanced by the large diatomite mine that has been operating for nearly fifty years.

This ranch has remained a haven in a world of turmoil, where peace and contentment can be found, and where nature's way prevails over much of the land. May it prevail for many more generations.

Rancho San Julian:
A History

San Julián Ranch

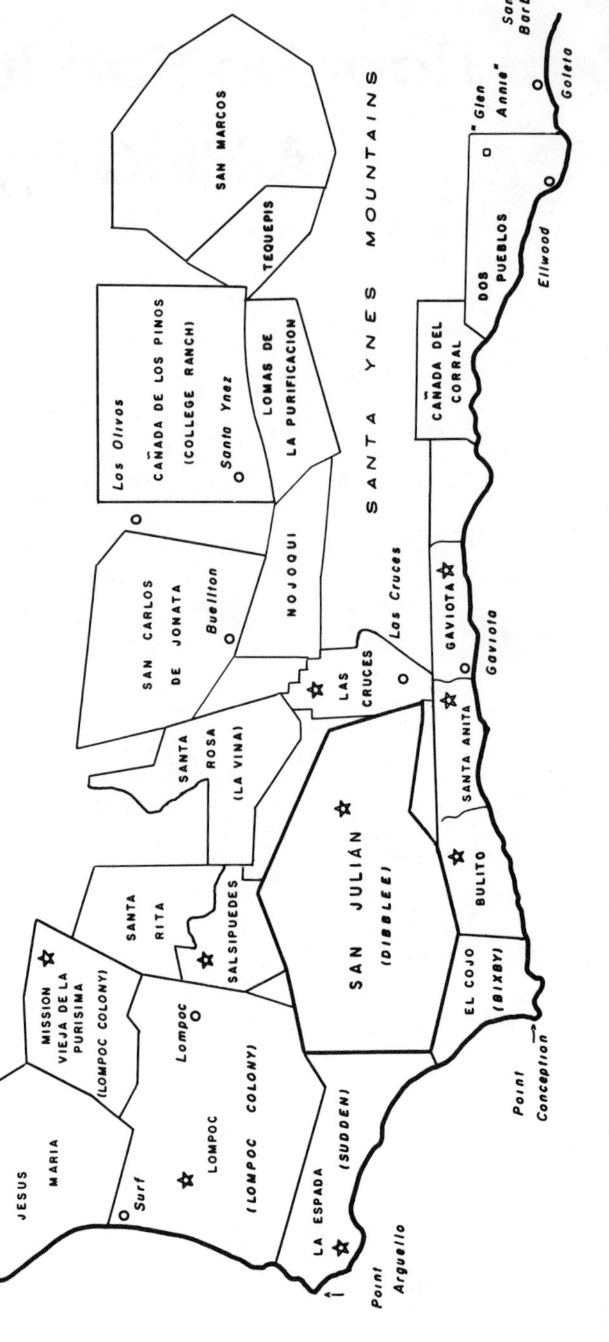

Location and Topography

RANCHO San Julian is located in southwestern Santa Barbara County, not far from the sea, where the Santa Ynez mountains evolve into the Santa Rosa Hills, whose escarpment ridge overlooks the Santa Ynez River Valley. From there the hills slope gently westward and southwestward to the valley floor of San Julian. The hills on the south side rise more abruptly to form the valley, which is the outstanding topographical feature of San Julian, extending the whole way through the ranch and bisecting it into virtually equal parts.

About two miles down from the top of Las Cruces grade, a large *barranca* (gully) appears and extends the rest of the way through San Julian and beyond. It has been said that this *barranca* was formed in the extremely wet winter of 1861–62, when the San Joaquin Valley was inundated and the water rose to the tops of the telegraph poles. Before that time, it was said that a rider could jump the stream on horseback, as we still can do in parts of Los Yridises.

Near the place where the *barranca* starts, the mountain range to the south intrudes the valley and extends for about a mile toward the west

3

The earliest known photograph of San Julian Valley was taken around 1875, looking northwest. Casa San Julian can be seen in the upper right with a barn and other outbuildings. Only the central section and west wing of the house appear, as the east wing was not added until 1878.

and then veers off sharply to the south nearly opposite the Casa, which is about midway down the valley.

At the point where the mountain comes close to the *barranca*, where the Gaviotita and Pacífico faults converge, there is a geological overturn. Along the ridge to the west, the mountain assumes a more rugged and rocky countenance, and the heavy and coarse sandstone is exposed. Further along, where it turns more on edge, Wilson Dibblee engaged the late Joseph Hollister (of the family who owned the adjacent Hollister Ranch) to drill two horizontal wells into the coarse sandstone ridge, with the result that the range was tapped for the benefit of the Casa. The water so produced flows down a pipeline to a point virtually across

San Julian Valley as it appears today, looking southeast toward the Santa Rosa Hills, with Casa San Julian in the center and the San Julian Road (California Highway 1) to the right.

the *barranca*, crosses that gulch, then flows up the hill to a reservoir high above the house. This is an example of the foresight and good planning Wilson Dibblee used to ensure the viability of the ranch, for the springs to the north, which once supplied the house, have virtually dried up due to land slippage.

There is little chance of finding water by drilling on the bottom lands of San Julian, for the valley is fairly steep and narrow and not conducive to the formation of gravel and sand acquifers, such as are found in the big broad valleys, nor is there an abundance of sand or gravel in the upper reaches of San Julian to form such acquifers.

As previously indicated, the Casa and headquarters of San Julian are located approximately halfway down the valley on the north side of the large *barranca* and are nestled against the gently sloping hills to the north, which rise to the geodetic monument, "Rosa," on Los Yridises. The house is close to a creek (one of the three flowing out of the hills to the northeast) and a small canyon, which we named Sneeze Canyon.

Here the valley floor is about a mile wide. The mountain range to the south distances itself from the level land and is less steep as it trends northwestward. The wide alluvial plain of black adobe extends for about two miles to the northwest, where the hills to the north and south again come closer to the valley floor. Over the low range to the west there is a hidden valley we call Los Amoles, named for the lily whose bulb gives off a soapy lather, and was used by the Indians. This hidden valley begins in the southwesternmost high hills of San Julian, next to Jalama and the Hollister Ranch, where the rainfall is the heaviest on the ranch. This valley trends northwestward for about three miles, finally joining the main creek of San Julian at the entrance to El Jaro.

Because of the difficulty of bridging a gulch, the old road through San Julian remained mostly on the northerly side of the large *barranca*. The *barranca* winds its way down, finally coming to a gorge at Los Palos Colorados. This *barranca* consists of about one hundred and fifty acres of wasteland heavily populated by willow, cottonwood, baccharis, nettles, blackberries, *hierba buena*, various species of bushes and grasses, among which are the *melilotus alba* and the *melilotus officiianalis* (sour clover), and a myriad other plants. This provides a fine wildlife refuge for the animals of the region, many of which come out to feed in the evening from their cool hiding places to browse on the beans and sudan grass, or to partake of the fruit or vegetables from the garden at the Casa.

To the east of Los Amoles and commencing at the top of a ridge there is piece of land that slopes southeastward toward the sea. This place was a parcel lying between the boundaries of the Rancho San Julian and Rancho Nuestra Señora del Refugio of Captain José Francisco Ortega (which were assumed to be adjacent, but were determined by government survey to be about a mile apart). The land was filed upon by the Dibblees. They then deeded an undivided interest to Hollister. In the

Pacífico Ortega House, ca. 1900

division of the two ranches between the parties, the ownership of that parcel was assumed by the Dibblees. In the original filing for ownership by the Dibblees, they were preceded by a man named Pacífico Ortega, who had filed for one hundred and sixty acres near the canyon bottom. He lived there the rest of his life. After his death, his widow sold his portion to the Dibblees, and the piece was named El Pacífico. This canyon is quite steep and very rocky on the northerly side, where the large sandstone ridge separates that portion from the San Julian Valley.

There is a large timber belt in the central portion of the canyon, and a stream that begins near the top and forms a small creek down the canyon's center. Only about a third of the land is clear and good for grazing, but the feed there is fairly rich. The creek flows into the Hollister Ranch at a narrow gorge in the bottom of the canyon, and there is a fairly high ridge to the south, where the land of the Hollister Ranch meets our land.

The de la Guerras

AS CHILDREN raised in Santa Barbara about a mile from the house of our great-great-grandfather, José de la Guerra, we had been coming to Rancho San Julian since (for me) time immemorial. As we grew older, we heard stories of our ancestors in Spain and were shown pictures of their houses and castles, together with the family escutcheon (or *escudos*, as they are called in Spanish). Family heirlooms proclaimed the antiquity of the Noriega and de la Guerra families.

The Noriega escutcheon bore the legend "Angelus Pelayo Nunciat sus Victoriam," referring to a man named Pelayo who led his troops to a victory over the conquering Muslims at the battle of Covadonga in 815. Pelayo went on to form a kingdom in the Asturias, around which the sturdy northerners rallied and which ultimately became the Kingdom of Castille. The invaders never were able to gain ascendancy over that region of Spain.

Likewise, the de la Guerra family was renowned for the number of its members who fought for imperial Spain against the Muslims and in regions such as Lepanto and Pavia and in the Netherlands.

Were these stories fact or legend? My sister Frederica and I determined to find out once and for all, so we set out for Spain in the spring of 1972. This was my fourth trip to Spain and her fifth, but it was the first

Noriega family coat of arms, or escudo.

time we seriously sought out our roots in that country. It is true that the groundwork for our quest had been laid nearly sixty years before when our cousin Serena Oreña and her brother Orestes traveled there in 1910 and commissioned extensive genealogical studies. But the results were not published for many years and remained obscure to us, although photographs of the Palacio Torre de la Guerra in Ibio and Casa Noriega in Llanes were among our family heirlooms.

Our objective was to see first-hand these ancient dwellings and the birthplace of Don José de la Guerra in the village of Novales (which we failed to find) and to obtain documentation on the de la Guerra and Noriega genealogy from the Archivos de Santander. The Spanish, like the British, are great record keepers and many of their records reach back into antiquity.

We rented a car in Lisbon and drove to Algecires, then on to Seville and Madrid. We made an unhurried trip north, where we arrived rested at the border town of Irun, still a long way from our objective. Soon we were on our way to Bilbao, in the Bass (or low) Pyrenees.

The low Pyrenees contributed to the treacherous road along the sea coast, which slowed us down (though the natives whizzed by as though the devil were after them), and the churning seas below reached up at us like a dragon seeking its prey. Few guard rails protected the motorist from a drop into the roiling waters. We were glad to leave those curves behind.

The mountains disappeared as we approached Santander, the beautiful city on a peninsula overlooking a bay and, further, the sea, much as San Francisco is situated in California. It took us a drive of five long miles to cross the estuary, which was too wide to bridge near the sea. We approached the city from the west on a broad avenue lined with poplar and plane trees, typical of the city's avenues.

We procured rooms at a fine hotel that used to be the Royal Palace. The floor and columns were of marble and the rooms spacious, as would befit royal quarters. There we rested and made plans for the following day.

We sought a guide who might be able to take us to the Noriega house and the family dwelling at Ibio, where the de la Guerras had founded their mayorazgo (or entailed estates) in the early fourteenth century.[1]

On the following day, a drive along the avenue took us to the Spanish travel bureau, where we hired a guide to take us around the country. The handsome Doña Helena Gonzales-Pardo, to our great astonishment and delight, knew the Noriega family. In fact, she had given music lessons to their children, and told us that the head of the household, Don Eduardo Noriega, had recently retired from the ministry of railroads, and that the family, who had a residence in Santander, at the moment was at their summer house in the village of Colombres, about eighty miles away. Doña Helena also knew of the priest at the village of Oreña.

We contacted the priest by telephone and he agreed to accompany us on our voyage the next day. The padre, whose name was David Rabre, presided at the church at Orenã, which had been endowed by our cousin

Arturo Oreña when he went to Spain in the early part of the century with his wife, Caroline Redmond of New York. On a subsequent trip there with his second wife, Elvira Mejia, Arturo died and his remains were sent back to California for burial.

The town of Oreña was but a few miles from Novales, where José de la Guerra was born. A cousin of ours, Eduardo de Koch, had asked me to go to the town of Oreña and see if Palacio Oreña still stood. Oddly enough, as I was strolling around on a new building site at Santillana del Mar, I saw some stones and asked where they were from. I was informed that they were from the Palacio Oreña, which had been torn down! They were to be incorporated into the façade for a new *albergue* (hotel), which the buyer planned to construct at Santillana del Mar, near the caves of Altamira.

As noted elsewhere in this narrative, Gaspar Oreña followed José de la Guerra to Santa Barbara and married De la Guerra's daughter, María Antonia.

Our drive the next day took us along the coastal plain and across a river to the bustling city of Torrelavega, then about thirty miles farther to Santillana del Mar. A short distance from there was Oreña, where we found the priest who we had contacted the previous day ready to accompany us on our trip. He was a man of about forty, dressed in mufti, as is the custom in Spain and France, where members of the clergy are not allowed to wear their robes in public. David Rabre was genial and talkative, but not overly so. He answered our questions but was careful not to say anything derogatory about the Franco regime, as were many others we met. This reluctance to criticize Franco stemmed from the long years of oppression and censorship, and many were fearful lest their utterances reach unfriendly ears. There was an apprehension of the future of Spain after Franco's death, as it was widely believed that Spain, virtually bankrupt in self-government, would be unable to handle the freedom necessary to a democratic society.

Leaving Oreña, we drove west across the virtually treeless pastures with little farming and few orchards. Occasionally we saw some small orange orchards, but the climate is not hot enough to ripen this fruit well, and the frequent rains of summer probably discourage farming of grains on a large scale. We did observe large groves of eucalyptus on some of the steep hillsides. These trees are cut back after about twenty years or so and the cut wood used for the manufacture of rayon. The trees, we were told, could be cut back three times before having to be replaced. I wondered what the results to the soil would be after such a program.

This northern region of Spain had been, for many centuries, used for grazing sheep. The export of wool to the Netherlands, which started around the sixteenth century, had been an important source of revenue for Spain; it had been decreed that the sheep industry of Castille was of paramount interest to the country and should not be interfered with.[2] Sheep from the north were allowed to pasture in the warmer southern regions during winter, and grazed on the way to and from their northern habitat. The predominating breed of sheep, merinos, produced a quality of wool superior to any other in Europe (save perhaps the angora wool of the goat). The merinos had been introduced into Spain by the African Berbers during the early part of the Muslim occupation, about the ninth or tenth century.[3] The Spaniards tried to confine the proliferating sheep, but the herds soon spread to others parts of Europe. Because of the damp climate, the merino sheep did not thrive on the British Isles.

The scarcity of trees in the northern region, and indeed over much of Spain, seems to have stemmed from the early Roman occupation of Spain, about 150 B.C., when Carthage was driven out and the Romans took over the immensely rich gold-producing country. It has been written that the Romans discovered large deposits of gold in·the Asturias, and it has been estimated that the Romans, who had previously relied on silver as a means of coinage, processed from 20 million to 30 million tons of rock to extract gold in that region. In order to mine and smelt this amount of ore, large amounts of timber were necessary to shore up the tunnels and smelt the ores. This denuding of the forests of Spain continued for at least seven hundred years, not only in the north but in other areas where gold was found.[4] It has been estimated that perhaps 500 million tons of rock or ore was processed by the Romans in their quest for gold. Pliny stated that the rivers of Spain were reduced to channels of silt that transported the residue to the sea. On discovering gold in a mountain, the Romans would often tunnel into that mountain, shoring the tunnel with timber. Then they would sluice away the top with water, often brought there from a great distance, until the water seeped into the tunnel. Slaves were then required to knock out the props of the tunnel. As they ran for the safety of the tunnel's mouth, they were often trapped by the falling mountain. One can imagine the staggering amount of timber needed to smelt the huge amounts of ore. The deforesting of the northern regions of the country very likely resulted in a drastic change in the climate and rainfall in the rest of the country.

Another feature of this northern part of Spain is the turbulence of the ocean on the Bay of Biscay. Having been born virtually on the shores of the Pacific and reared not more than two miles from the sea, and having lived virtually all of my adult life within ten miles of the ocean, I can appreciate the meaning of the word "pacific," for the waters of the Bay of Biscay are the roughest, most turbulent I have ever seen. The waves, buffeted by the winds blowing across this large body of water, are of tremendous size and seem to originate a long way out to sea, perhaps as much as a mile or so. They come thundering onto the shore one after the other in a frightening cadence that would intimidate even the strongest swimmers. Indeed, on one trip in the region, we saw a swimmer swept out to sea and very nearly drowned. Even at the Bay of San Jean-de-Luz, where the rip tides are at a minimum, we were tossed about relentlessly by the huge breakers. The hardiest of fishermen have great respect for the roiling waters, and many a fishing boat has been capsized there. We saw no pleasure craft along the coast.

Casa Noriega

We proceeded from Oreña across the treeless plain for several miles before turning inland to the rolling hills, where we encountered the village of Colómbres, where the Noriegas lived. Their house was nestled in a grove of sycamore and poplar. The town was situated around a large square on which was located a park.

The Noriega house, on the northwest edge of the square, was a large,

Torre Noriega in Llanes, Spain, was constructed in about the eighth century.

two-story, wooden structure under the overhanging sycamores. Getting out of our car, we approached the house, where we saw some people sitting on a veranda. They immediately recognized our guide, Doña Helena, and the children ran to her embrace. After proper introductions, reinforced by the padre, the Noriega cousins entertained us warmly. Their astonishment knew no bounds, since the California branch of the family had practically disappeared into obscurity one hundred and fifty years before. They brought out the family escutcheon, which we recognized immediately, and whose motto ("Angelus Pelayo Nunciat sus Victoriam") I quoted to them even before reading the inscription. The family's connection to Pelayo is uncertain, but the Noriegas' long adherence to this legend gives the appearance of some credence. (Strangely enough, as we later discovered, Señorita Tapia's father and Don Noriega were acquainted and both had worked in the ministry of transportation in Madrid.)

Reluctantly taking leave of our newfound cousins, we headed south into the hills of the Asturias and soon encountered the hamlet of Noriega, with its stone-towered castles situated on a windswept hill. There was little activity and absolutely no traffic to be seen. The towers, which seemed to have been well constructed of stone, were round and fairly large—about forty feet in diameter and forty or fifty feet in height. There were small lookout windows near the top where the occupants could see any menacing marauder or enemy. The escutcheons were at least twenty feet from the ground, but nearly all of them so damaged by the elements as to be illegible. At one of these buildings we stopped to ask the way to Torre Noriega and were subjected to a long line of questioning by an old lady who probably had not seen a stranger for a decade. Finally, we were told where Torre Noriega was, but that the owner was away in Madrid, and so we would not see the interior of the place.

Torre de la Guerra

Our next destination was the town of Ibio, situated in the Valle del Cabezón. This was where the de la Guerras had founded their mayorazgo and Solar de Ibio in the fourteenth century, and where they had endowed a church named La Iglesia del Consejo de Ibio, which had a special dispensation from the Pope.[5]

Torre de la Guerra in Ibio, Spain, was built in the fourteenth century.

De la Guerra escutcheon at Torre de la Guerra in Ibio, Spain

David Rabre had been to Ibio before, and readily found the local priest, who agreed to show us Palacio Torre de la Guerra. He gave no clue as to the condition of the building, but kept us on tenterhooks as we made our slow way down the streets of the town. We had come nearly six thousand miles to see this place and we could hardly restrain our impatience, which he seemed to nurture. "The house will still be there when we arrive. Patience my children," he said.

As we rounded a turn in the street, there loomed a large, four-story stone building with castellated parapets along the sloping roof. We knew that we had at last reached our goal. The imposing structure stood just as depicted in ancient drawings and old photographs, except that a roof leaning toward a wall on the east side had been added who knows

De la Guerra family coat of arms, or escudo

when. Under this roof we saw an escutcheon high on the outer wall, but could not read the inscription. With the help of a ladder procured from the caretaker, I climbed high enough to photograph the ornament—the first one we had ever seen covered and protected from the elements. I could not read the inscription, which was in Gothic script. Another motto ("Ave Maria Gratia Plena") had come into the de la Guerra family with the marriage of Gonzalo Guerra to Ynez de la Vega, when the Vega Mayorazgo was truncated due to the absence of a male heir in the Vega family.

For twelve generations thereafter, the eldest son of the de la Guerras of Ibio assumed the matronym of Vega or de la Vega after the Guerra name, this because the Vega family was the more prominent in national recognition. Garcillaso de la Vega, a cousin of Ynez, had been Adelantado Mayor de Castilla, or chief justice in time of peace and head of the armed forces in time of war.

Peter the Cruel was king of Castilla at the time, and his brutality was notorious. He resented the power and popularity of Garcillaso de la Vega and ordered his death, whereupon Peter's henchmen bludgeoned the hapless statesman to death and tossed his body out of a building onto the Plaza de Toros at Burgos. This occurred in the mid-fourteenth century, and was chronicled by Pedro Lopez de Ayala in his *Crónicas de los Reyes de Castilla*.

The Guerras of Ibio prospered and their land holdings increased to the extent that they owned land from Ibio to Santander (but not in contiguous parcels), and maintained residences in both cities.

From Ibio and Santander, the Guerras sallied forth to fight for imperial Spain in such numbers over the centuries as to evoke a comment from one Augustin Rodriguez Fernandes, that

> [I]n the historical judgment of this house [family], we wonder above all at the marvellous fitness of its members to the etymological significance of the name. It seems to follow that the term "Guerra" exerted on the representatives of this family an inner irresistible determination, almost genetic, that marked them with the cast of warriors. Race of Captains; we can say without any exaggeration whatsoever that there was scarcely a battle with Imperial Spain in which a Guerra was not represented. Among the "clusters" of their military service are the names of Granada, Pavia, Lepanto, and Flanders.

The first of these Guerras seems to have been Captain Diego Guerra, who fought and died at the battle of Granada in 1492, the last Muslim stand in Spain. Also in that battle were Sergeant-Major Gonzalo Guerra and young Pedro Guerra, the captain of Caballos Corrazas.

In the sixteenth century, we find Gonzalo Guerra de la Vega, Señor de la Casa in Ibio, as *veedor* (inspector general) of the Spanish contingent that formed a part of the armada that defeated the Turks at Lepanto in 1561.[6] That armada, which contained a fleet that came mainly from Venice, was commanded by the Provitodore Barbagio; the Pope's squadron was under the command of Marcantonio Collona, a prominent Roman whose descendants still live in that city. The Neopolitan contingent was commanded by the marqueses of Santa Cruz and Cordona, Spanish officers.

The Turkish fleet comprised 273 light galleys and was in command of the Ali Pasha; the allied fleet comprised 200 galleys and eight "galleases" (heavy galleys). The two fleets met in long lines off Cape Scropha on October 7, 1561. The Turks were more lightly armed, still depending on bow and arrow and light cannon, while the allies were armed with heavier guns and muskets on their larger galleys. The ships of Ali Pasha and Don Juan of Austria, who was in overall command of the allied fleet, met prow to prow; the former's ship was boarded and he was killed. The Turks were utterly routed despite a successful maneuver by Ulich Aly, whose ships penetrated the line when Giandrea Doria, thinking he would be outflanked, stood out to sea, but the gap created was quickly filled by the Marques of Santa Cruz, who was being held in reserve for just such a contingency. The loss to the Turks was estimated to be at twenty thousand, while the allies lost about six thousand men. This decisive defeat of the Turks at Lepanto put an end to the threat of further Moslem invasion of Europe, and it has been said that the Turks undoubtedly could have mounted a counter-offensive but that they did not do so on account of their preoccupation with the conquest of Persia.

Others killed in the Battle of Lepanto were the prominent Turk Sicorro and the Barbagio of Venice, and among the wounded was Miguel Cervantes, who took a bullet in the left hand, which was thereafter immobilized, as he later quipped, "for the greater glory of my right." G.K. Chesterton later wrote:

> Cervantes on his galley sets his sword back in its sheath;
> Don Juan of Austria rides homeward with a wreath,
> and he sees across a weary land a straggling road in Spain
> up which a lean and foolish knight forever rides in vain.
> And he smiles but not as sultans smile, and settles back the blade
> (But Don Juan of Austria rides home from the Crusade).

Two previous Guerras, both named Gonzalo, participated in battle—one at Pavia and one as contador in Flanders,[7] dates unknown. Then there was Don Juan de la Guerra Vega who, as captain of infantry in Flanders, received wounds at the Battle of Namour from which he died in the home of a lady of Brussels who had nursed him.[8] That battle was a desperate attempt by Don Juan of Austria, who had succeeded the Duke of Alba as commander of Spanish troops in Flanders, to quell the mutiny among the troops who, on account of Spain's bankruptcy, had not been paid for some time. The promise of loot from the well-fortified citadel prompted super-human efforts from those troops, who finally overcame the defenders and sacked the place. Don Juan of Austria made Namour his headquarters in Flanders and later died there.[9]

Don Juan de la Guerra, in a long and detailed will, left many bequests, one of which was a generous gift to the Belgian lady. Another of his wishes provided that a silver lamp of his, then in the possession of a tailor in Brussels as security for some work done for the captain, be redeemed and sent back to Ibio, where it should be placed next to the Blessed Sacrament, and that oil for the lamp should be provided in "perpetuity" from his estate.[10] But alas! His estate had been squandered by his son, who was supposed to care for his father's property in his absence, and there was not enough to pay much of the bequests. The church mentioned in his will no longer existed by the time we arrived there, and the parish priest was surprised that we even knew about the church so long forgotten.

The seventeenth century also witnessed another Guerra, Don Fernando de la Guerra Vega,[11] who was also Señor de la Casa at Ibio. He was commander of the garrison and governor of Santander, his dwelling place. He made out his will and died in 1679.

In the late eighteenth century, while in Mexico City, José de la Guerra y Noriega joined the army of Spain[12], and in the early nineteenth century he fought for Spain against the insurgents at the battle of Tejpic in 1811.[13] This brought to an end the long list of Guerras who fought for Spain, with the possible exception of a de la Guerra whom we were told about in Novales, who went to the Philippines and fought in the Spanish-American War, but this has not been authenticated.

The de la Guerra dynasty at Ibio lasted until 1748, when Ignacio Guerra of Ibio died without leaving any sons, and his eldest daughter, who had married Francisco Javier de Ceballos,[14] inherited the Mayorazgo and Solar of Ibio, which had been in the Guerra family for 445 years. Full circle had come the Guerra and Ceballos families since Gonzalo Guerra married Rosenda Ceballos in the early thirteenth century, and now the Ceballos were the "señores" of Ibio.

By that time, one of the younger sons of Gonzalo Guerra de la Vega and his second wife, who did not participate in the inheritance at Ibio, had established his own Mayorazgo of Novales and Mazuercas. Those estates went down to Juan de la Guerra,[15] who married María Teresa Noriega, to whom was born, in the village of Novales, a son they named José Antonio Julian.

The New World

By the time José was thirteen years of age, trouble was brewing in Europe following the French Revolution, and it is likely that José's parents decided to send the lad off to America on that account, where Don Pedro Noriega, the brother of José's mother, maintained a successful commercial establishment in Mexico City.[16] The following year, 1793, Spain was invaded by France.

To a lad brought up in the provincial village of Novales, life in Mexico City must have been a challenging and invigorating experience, and he quickly learned his uncle's business. To return to Spain was unthinkable for an ambitious lad who undoubtedly saw the opportunities opening in the frontiers of this new world. So, at the age of eighteen, José joined the army of Spain. This disappointed Don Pedro, who had hoped the bright and likeable lad would join his own enterprise.[17]

In a day when influence and family background were important factors in a young man's advancement, José de la Guerra had the edge over many of his contemporaries. His father's uncle was minister of war in Madrid (the practice of excluding men of the upper classes from high places in government having gone by the boards in the intervening three hundred years since Isabel had instituted the policy). José had the faculty of making friends in high places, which is not to imply that he was not capable. In fact, his next advancement to lieutenant and *habilitado* (paymaster) at Monterey in Alta California came about because, as his good friend Don Manuel Caracaba, *habilitado* of the Californias, stated, "José was a very good accountant."[18]

José left Mexico in February 1801 for that "distant Siberia," as California was sometimes referred to, and did not reach Monterey until August.

Don Raimundo Carrillo left the command at Monterey after four years to assume command at Santa Barbara,[19] and he departed thence with his wife and beautiful daughter, María Antonia, several months after José's arrival, but not before de la Guerra and the girl had fallen in love. Permission to marry had to be obtained, not only from the parents and the church, but also from the king. The nearly six-month-long process of obtaining this permission culminated in the marriage of José and María Antonia Carrillo at the mission in Santa Barbara on May 16, 1804.[20] As has been customary in the Spanish army to this day, it was necessary for an officer, due to the meager salary paid in the army, to furnish proof of outside income. José was able to do this with help from the commercial enterprise he conducted with his uncle in Mexico. In fact, José de la Guerra continued his commercial business most of his life, and in the process was able to support a large family in a manner befitting his rank. His outside income also helped to pay the troops of the Presidio when the government ran short of funds, as frequently happened, so that when he received his grant to San Julian, the government owed him approximately $12,000.

Upon the departure of Raimundo Carrillo, the post at Monterey was left vacant, and José's good friend, Arrillaga, appointed him temporary commander there, a position he executed so satisfactorily that Arrillaga then nominated him for comandante at Santa Barbara on the retirement of Carrillo four years later.[21]

He did not receive that appointment, however, and Arrillaga wrote him a letter expressing his disappointment at this turn of events.[22] José's next assignment was to the Santa Barbara company with service to be performed at San Diego. Shortly after his arrival there he became embroiled with a fellow officer of equal rank who claimed that he, and not de la Guerra, should assume temporary command at that post. De la Guerra pointed out that when two officers of equal rank arrived at a post, it was customary for the first one to arrive to take command, but the other fellow insisted that the position was his, and the two young hotheads drew swords and prepared to fight it out. However, they were dissuaded from that course by fellow officers and were severely reprimanded by their superiors, who reminded them that such action could result in dismissal or, worse, court-martial. The two were assigned to different posts and shortly thereafter, as an indication of their confidence in him, de la Guerra was elected by the California army officers to be *habilitado general*[23] of the Californias, and in August 1810 the governor of California ordered him to proceed to Mexico City.

According to Joseph Thompson in his book, *El Gran Capitán*, de la Guerra's passport was dated August 31, 1810, and "he departed with his family and brother-in-law, Carlos Carrillo, from San Diego to San Blás, on the brig *Santissima Virgen*, but did not reach Mexico City because, on his arrival at San Blás, the ship was captured by insurgents under Mercado, a partisan of Hidalgo" during the Mexican revolution at Guanaguato in 1810. Thompson goes on to state that (according to Vallejo) "de la Guerra was sentenced to be executed [on account of his Spanish birth] on September 15th." That date, however, is in error, since the revolution begun under the leadership of Hidalgo and Allende, and still celebrated as Mexican independence day, did not begin until September 16.[24] This happened in the village of Dolores, some three hundred miles from San Blás,[25] therefore the message is not likely to have been transmitted to San Blás on the same day.

De la Guerra's refusal to acknowledge the revolutions in Mexico and the rest of Spanish America appears to be a commentary on his blind loyalty toward his native Spain.[26] Nor would he even discuss the matter, for we find almost no reference in letters regarding these important events, although he did discuss events in Europe and Napoleon's successes on the continent.[27]

Revolution from Spain brought a relaxation of trade restrictions

The Santa Barbara adobe house of José de la Guerra as it appeared around the turn of the century. Casa de la Guerra, built in the 1820s, was the center of social and political life in the pueblo. The two-story altito *can be seen in the upper right.*

imposed by the Spaniards, and this enabled de la Guerra to expand his trade in merchandise with the aid of his uncle, Don Pedro Noriega of Mexico City, with whom he had maintained relations since his departure there twenty years before.

He purchased a vessel in which he had goods brought from San Blás, the most important west coast port at the time. He traded with whoever had goods for sale, sometimes taking notes specifying that he would be paid in cattle when the time came to collect. He seemed always to have had gold to use for his purchases, as many travelers who visited de la Guerra recounted stories of the great amounts of gold he had stored in his *altito,* (little tower). There is a story that some of his sons would occasionally climb onto the roof and remove a tile and lower a string on which a glob of tar was stuck to lift out a gold piece or two, until the miscreants were caught at it. However, much of this gold belonged to the mission padres, who had traded hides and tallow for gold, and de la Guerra was the keeper of their treasure. He would never use any of their gold for his own use. His use of "promise to pay" in heifers came in good

*Capitan José Antonio Julián de la Guerra y Noriega, grantee of
Rancho San Julian and comandante of the Santa Barbara Presidio, as
painted by Leonardo Barbieri in 1856.*

stead, for when he acquired his many ranches, he needed cattle to stock
them, and sometimes called in those notes.[28]

Much of the silverware, utensils, clothing, household furniture, and
myriad other goods came from Mexico, Chile, Peru, and the East Coast
of the United States, as practically none of these was made in California.
The Manila galleons that passed California for two hundred and fifty
years were not allowed to trade with the Californians, as the goods
were destined for the richer markets of Mexico, where such luxuries as
silk, fine furniture, or expensive jewelry could be sold at a better price.[29]

De la Guerra's trade was mostly local, except when his ship passed certain southern California ports, nor did he travel much along El Camino Real.

Ah, what magic those words—El Camino Real—conjure up: Visions of handsome carriages drawn by prancing horses and carrying beautifully coiffed ladies accompanied by dashing caballeros in splendid attire with outriders at postillion. But nothing could be further from the truth, for El Camino Real generally referred to the trails or paths followed by the padres on foot, or by riders traveling between missions, such as the trail over the San Marcos Pass, or the trail between La Purísima Vieja and the new mission in Lompoc Valley. The term King's Highway was first used in the Old Testament, and dated to the time when Moses asked (but was denied) permission to pass over the King's Highway.[30]

According to the late Reverend Maynard Geiger, El Camino Real continued up the coast through the Gaviota ranch of Francisco Ortega to a place where a pass in the low ridge led down San Miguelito canyon to Mission Purísima Vieja. Apparently there was no passable road through the Gaviota pass, since W.W. Hollister told about having to dismantle his wagon and carry it across the Gaviota creek when he passed that way in 1854.[31] There were no bridges spanning the wide California rivers, for those would have been a challenge even for the Romans, who were bridge builders, as the Californians were not.

Hattie Stone Benefield of the Foxen family wrote of crossing the Santa Ynez River while in flood. She said the vaqueros of the Mission Santa Inés were enlisted to help the stagecoach cross the river by fastening riatas to the coach from both sides of the river so that it would not drift away in the heavy flood, and that the coach being water-tight acted like a boat and floated across.[32]

On the southern approach to Santa Barbara, the Rincon was passable only at low tide, and the Conejo grade south of Ventura was so steep that passengers often told of having to drag a tree or log behind the stage in order to keep it from running away. What kind of a King's Highway was that?

California's economy during the Spanish period was relatively stagnant as there was little trade, except in hides, horns, and tallow, and the government maintained a tariff of a hundred percent on goods that were imported. This led to a considerable amount of smuggling. About the only exception was the otter trade. Yankees, however, were adept smugglers, and there was no fleet of coastal ships to intercept them.[33]

With independence from Spain in 1822, these strict rules were relaxed and tariff imposts were lowered, allowing more goods to flow into Alta California. Then the trade in hides and tallow increased and continued until the missions were secularized in the mid-1830s, at which time a liberal policy of land grants was instituted, removing much of the land from the control of the missions.

De la Guerra took advantage of every opportunity that came his way to turn an honest penny. He realized the need for beef by the increasing number of ships passing his way. He was always ready to supply their needs for fresh beef from cattle on his Conejo ranch, south of Ventura, and later from San Julian, for which he arranged a slaughter yard in Santa Barbara.

By the time of the Louisiana Purchase in 1803 and Texas' independence from Mexico in 1836 and its acquisition by the U.S. in 1845, the United States' expanding borders were suddenly thrust up against those of Mexico, with the inevitable result of conflict between the two countries.

Governor Juan Bautista Alvarado saw the movement of the colossus of the north and determined that California would soon be in the hands of that country. He accelerated a program of land grants in Alta California so that most of the land would already be in the hands of his countrymen when the Yankees came.[34]

During the Spanish regime, only about twenty-five land grants had been made in California. These were provisional grants, destined to revert to the Spanish crown.[35] There were perhaps just as many grants made by Mexican governors before Alvarado, but he and his lieutenant governor, Manuel Jimeno, made about two hundred land grants in the four years he was governor. Alvarado, however, had a severe drinking problem, and his administration was often in the hands of Jimeno.[36]

Very few of the Spanish grants survived the transition from Spanish to Mexican control.[37] Most of them expired and only a few were regranted by Mexican governors to the original grantee.[38] Some of those were validated by the U.S. Land Commission and some were denied validation.

A bitter feud had developed between Juan Alvarado, who had seized power in Monterey, and Carlos Carrillo, de la Guerra's brother-in-law, who had been named governor by the Mexican government. Carrillo had the support of only the *abajeños* (southern Californians), while Alvarado had a more numerous group of followers among the *arribeños* (northerners). Both Alvarado and Carrillo vied for de la Guerra's support, but he would not give overt support to either.[39] It is possible that Alvarado, by granting San Julian to de la Guerra and large grants of nearby lands to the Carrillo brothers, may have effectively neutralized any potentially powerful opposition, for he was later made de facto governor by the Mexican government when those authorities realized he had the upper hand.

When Alvarado's term of office expired (1842), he received in grant the 45,000-acre Mariposa Ranch on the Merced River in the San Joaquin Valley. He later sold the ranch to John C. Frémont. Several millions in gold were reportedly extracted after the hostile Indians of the region were put under control.[40]

The presidio in Santa Barbara accounted for about 150 officers and men at the time de la Guerra was granted San Julian,[41] and many of these men were mounted, since the presidio's jurisdiction extended from Mission Purísima in the west to Mission San Fernando in the east, a distance of about 150 miles. The area was patrolled on a more or less regular basis in order that the presidio commander could be apprised of events within his jurisdiction.

Early in 1824, there occurred an Indian uprising at Mission Purísima that spread rapidly to Santa Inés and Santa Barbara, and harsh measures were taken to quell the rebellion.[42] Historian Zephyrin Engelhardt and Reverend Geiger, both at Mission Santa Barbara, seemingly accused de la Guerra of negligence in controlling his soldiers when they killed some Indians and ransacked the Indian homes at the mission. Accounts by Hubert Howe Bancroft, Angustias de la Guerra, and Father Ripoll differ as to what caused the trouble. Historian H.E. Bolton further clouds the

During the Indian uprising of 1824, soldiers from the presidio killed innocent Indians and ransacked their homes at Mission Santa Barbara.

issue by stating that "in the writings of Engelhardt, one can detect where the historian stops and friar begins."[43] Nearly everyone, however, agreed that the troops were out of control when they broke into the Indian habitations, sacked them, and killed a number of apparently innocent Indians.[44] De la Guerra, since he was in overall command, must take the blame for the actions of his troops. Had he been present, those incidents could have been prevented.

De la Guerra engaged in the trade of otter skins, which seems to have netted him a bit of money, but how much or with whom he traded is not discernible. The official policy of the Spanish government was to give a monopoly on the sale of otter pelts to a man named Vasadre of San Blás, who had the concession with the Manila company to sell to the Chinese. This trade in otter pelts was flourishing in 1776, when Captain James Cook, stopping in China on his circumnavigation of the globe, reported the profitable trade in otter skins between the Russians and Chinese.

The Russians started trading in fine otter pelts from the Bering Sea.

When that area was depleted, they moved down the coast of North America and took large numbers of the animals with the aid of the Aleuts. These were excellent marksmen, and in their kayaks they could quietly approach the basking otters. The Russians were soon poaching along the southern coast of California, where pelts were inferior to those taken in colder waters.

The Americans and British soon got into the act with their whaling vessels. They established bases in the Antarctic, where they added seal skins to augment the diminishing supply of otter pelts.

The Americans were surprised to find that the Chinese used large numbers of Mexican silver pesos to pay for the furs. These coins, along with quicksilver, had been taken to the Philippines and China by the Manila galleons that traded with China by way of the Philippines. The Portuguese navigator Cermeno, sailing for Spain in the latter part of the sixteenth century, found that crossing the Pacific by way of the westward equatorial current and returning along the Japan current was quicker and more profitable than trying to beat against the prevailing westerly winds of the Pacific coast of California. The Spanish vessels sat high in the water and were short and square-rigged. In contrast, the British and American ships were relatively long and narrow and lay low in the water, and would tack into the wind with swinging jib booms. Thus the Spanish vessels could not take a strong wind to port or starboard without the risk of capsizing and so could not beat successfully against the wind. One account tells of sailing along the California coast and making headway of but three leagues in one day. It took de la Guerra six months to sail from San Blás to Monterey.

Adele Ogden, a critic of de la Guerra, accused him of engaging in trade with a smuggler named Eliab Grimes, against whom a "letter of marque" had been issued by the governor.[45] She recounted that a ship's log of Grimes's activities included an account of trading with de la Guerra at the time the letter was in effect, and that Grimes had sold goods to de la Guerra without the usual impost of duties. There is no mention of any sale or purchase of otter pelts, however, and the disposition of the pelts he acquired is unclear from a search of the archives. All this allegedly occurred while de la Guerra was in command at Santa Barbara.[46]

California Indians

The Spanish approach to dealing with the Indians was to Christianize and integrate them into Spanish society—this in contrast to the French and English penchant for either driving out the Indians or killing them. Perhaps the Indians living along the eastern American seaboard and the regions occupied by the French and British would never have accepted the system that the Indians of California did. California Indians were generally considered more peaceful.[47]

In general, de la Guerra's treatment of the Indians appears to have been stern but tempered with mercy when the occasion warranted, as in the case of some Indians who murdered a mayordomo at Mission San Diego. De la Guerra defended them by stating that while they were undoubtedly guilty, there was certainly great provocation because of the action of the mayordomo, who had abused his position by his conduct toward the Indians' wives.[48]

It is well to remember that the Spanish government in California was a military one, designed to cope with a potentially hostile population. The structure of that government had been carefully laid out by Felipe De Neve in the 1770's. He had meticulously specified how the government should function, laid out a series of post routes, and compiled a code of military conduct for the authorities to follow.[49] In 1774, the Spanish appointed De Neve to succeed Diego de Borica as California governor, which then included both Alta and Baja California.

The first order of business at each new outpost was the establishment of a presidio to protect civilians, clerics, and troops, and this was generally followed by attempts to make friends with the natives and to persuade them to assist in the construction of a mission. The Indians were often attracted by the offer of food and by the mystic nature of the church ritual, which appealed to their sense of the supernatural.

Governor De Neve was opposed to the enslavement of the Indians. Under the guidance of Father Junípero Serra, they were treated relatively kindly.[50] After Serra's death in 1784, abuses crept into the system at the prospects of large profits from the sale of hides and tallow augmented by forced Indian labor. This prompted some mission padres to force the

Indians to work by the threat and use of corporal punishment. The situation became so bad at Mission San Francisco that many Indians died; those who escaped were soon returned and punished. Governor Borica intervened on behalf of the Indians at San Francisco, and ordered the Franciscan friar Fermín Lasuén to desist from such treatment at that mission. The unworthy priest complained bitterly that without punishment the Indians could not be forced to work for them.[51]

Few now dispute that the Indians were subjected to involuntary servitude, but some of the missionaries justified their treatment of the Indians by contending that the Indians had known they were giving up their freedom when they came to the missions. Other writers of the time, such as Perfecto Hugo Reid, the Scotsman who married the beautiful Indian, Victoria, and gained possession of Rancho Santa Anita, admitted that slavery among the Indians did exist.[52] However, the 1825 letters of Fray Gonzalez de Ybarra to Carlos Carrillo indicate the friar's concern for the Indians, and state clearly that the Indians were subject to slavery and anyone disputing that assertion was resorting to lies and hypocrisy.[53] Letters from Ybarra to de la Guerra indicate the extent to which Indians were sent from one place to another under guard.

It appears to be about this time that the consciences of some of the padres and others in high authority in government were awakened to the evils of the system, for a letter from Arrillaga to de la Guerra commended him for giving liberty to a pagan Indian.[54] An 1821 letter to de la Guerra from Fray José Martinez of San Luis Obispo commended de la Guerra for preserving the freedom of some Indian slaves, and stated that "God will reward him despite the ingratitude of the Indians."

The high regard in which the padres held de la Guerra is manifested in a letter from Father Narcisso Durán, prior of the Santa Barbara Mission.[55] In a long letter to de la Guerra, Durán expressed his high admiration

> . . . for the great treasure of erudition which you have been able to
> acquire, but this is but to acknowledge that God has graced you with

the five talents of the Gospel, and your religious nature makes me hope
that you will know how to return to Him in equal number. . . .

The letter was a request that de la Guerra act as unofficial judge-
arbiter in a matter as to whether or not young Indian maidens, who had
come under the protection of the missionaries, should remain there or be
allowed to return to their families and resume their tribal customs.
Durán felt that the estrangement of these girls was a severe trial to both
themselves and their families. The implication was that, in any case,
when they finally returned to the tribes, the religious training they had
received would generally be lost to them. This seems to have been a tacit
admission of their failure to Christianize the Indian population.

None of this is to imply that de la Guerra was an abolitionist, or that
his concern for the Indians was attuned in that direction. It does attempt
to show a valid concern for the welfare of the native. It has been said that
de la Guerra had indentured Indians working for him in his house for
much of the time he lived in Santa Barbara. But this was before slavery
was abolished in the United States, and not long after such enlightened
Americans as Thomas Jefferson also kept slaves. Our judgment of those
people must be made within the context of their times.

De la Guerra was not, however, without his detractors, and it may
come as a distinct surprise to citizens of Santa Barbara, who are no
strangers to pollution, to learn that the leading citizen of the time was
accused of polluting a stream as early as 1839.

A man named Rojo[56] complained to the acting governor, Manuel
Jimeno, that a *matanza* operated by de la Guerra was fouling the waters
of a nearby stream, and the inhabitants below were inconvenienced by
the filth carried by the water from the slaughter of beef. De la Guerra, in
a reply to the official, admitted the existence of the slaughter yard, but
stated that the cattle were taken away from the stream early in the
morning so as to allow the impurities to flush away before the women
went out to wash. He did not concede that the stream was used as a
source of water to the inhabitants downstream. The resolution of the
dispute is not known, but de la Guerra agreed to obtain the services of a
butcher, which was supposed to abate some of the nuisance.

De la Guerra was scolded by one of the padres of the Santa Barbara

Mission for forsaking the ways of St. Francis in his use of a carriage.[57] He was a lay member of that order and, as such, was supposed to travel only on foot. It is presumed that his duties and trips from the presidio to the mission and the shore, where he maintained a warehouse, were too far, and thus took up too much of his time to travel by foot. Fray Martínez of San Luis Obispo used a horse-drawn carriage as well to cover the long distances he traveled.

De la Guerra Land Acquisitions

Captain José de la Guerra began acquiring land in 1822 with a grant by Governor Pablo Vicente de Solá to Rancho Conejo in what is now Ventura County.[58] This ranch had been provisionally granted to José Polanco and Ignacio Rodríguez, but with independence from Spain in 1822 that *repartimiento* grant expired and the portion previously held by Polanco was granted to de la Guerra. Rodríguez's part was regranted to him, but was ultimately acquired by de la Guerra. Now worth billions of dollars, the land was not particularly good as a cattle ranch, and its loss after de la Guerra's death was not greatly lamented by the family at the time.

A man named Joe Russell, who was a cousin of my brother-in-law, and who later became an owner of part of the ranch, told a story of how his father was traveling south on a stagecoach and became engaged in conversation with a fellow passenger. The man said he was headed for Rancho Conejo, which he intended to buy. He described in detail the location and other aspects of the ranch to Russell, who was also seeking a ranch to buy. At a stage stop along the way, Russell left the coach and hired the fastest horse available, arriving at the ranch in time to make a deal and greet the astounded coach passenger as the new owner. According to Russell, many western moving pictures have been shot there, and pictures of cattle drives were taken at roundup time when Hollywood needed some such action.[59]

Other de la Guerra acquisitions included San Julian, which was one of Alvarado's earliest grants, made on April 6, 1837.[60] This was the day

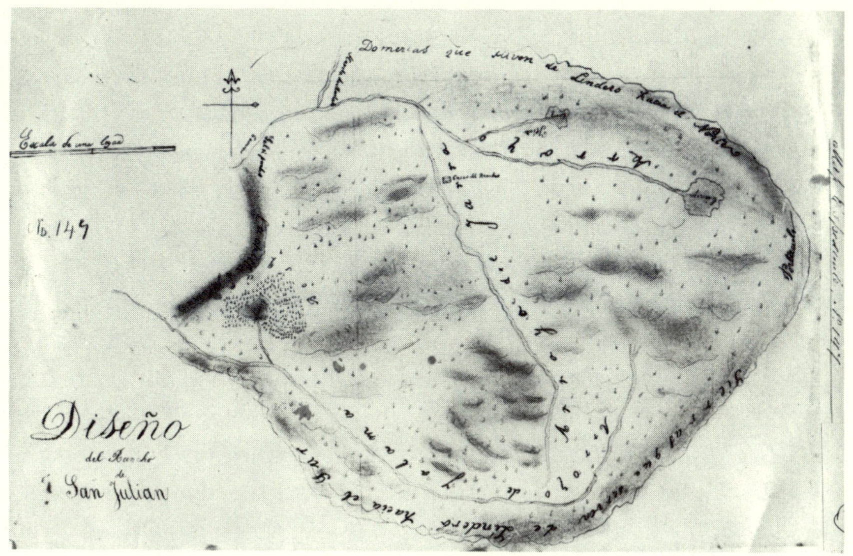

Early land grants were usually documented by crude maps called diseños *describing the property transferred, like this one for Rancho San Julian.*

after Alvarado granted Rancho Nipomo to William G. Dana, a relative of Richard Henry Dana, author of *Two Years Before the Mast.*

Rancho Simí was purchased in 1834 from Patricio Javier and Miguel Pico,[61] who were granted this 92,231-acre tract by Governor Borica in 1795, and which was revalidated by Alvarado in 1842. That ranch is in what is now some of the richest agricultural land in Ventura County, and was then used by de la Guerra and his sons as a cattle ranch. There is an account of how de la Guerra and a padre of Mission San Gabriel were poring over some records pertinent to Simí when someone at the mission became suspicious and reported to the governor that there was a conspiracy afoot. An arrest warrant was issued against de la Guerra, but he was able to prove to the satisfaction of the governor that he was concerned only about the matter of Simí, and he was exonerated. Later, the priest, Blás Ordaz, apologized to de la Guerra for the incident.

De la Guerra acquired the 25,000-acre Rancho Las Posas near Simí from José Carrillo, who was granted the ranch by Governor José Figueroa in 1834.[62] Leo Carrillo, in his book, *This California I Love,* recounted that the Carrillos were great gamblers, especially when it came to racing horses against their rivals, and he told of how they would wager even their ranches against an adversary in a horse race.[63] In this way, they lost much of their land. But it is extremely unlikely that Las Posas changed hands in that manner, for de la Guerra was not one to recklessly gamble away his hard-earned wealth.

With the coming of the Yankees in the late 1840's and early 1850's, there arose a demand for beef so strong that the price of cattle soared from about $5 to as much as $50 a head.[64] Seldom were ranchers in such a favorable position as the California cattlemen with a million cattle ready for sale, and the Californians took full advantage of the bonanza after Nicolas Den made a cattle drive to the north. This bonanza soon brought millions of cattle and sheep from Texas and the plains states, with a resulting drop in prices. Such drives, of course, became less profitable and less frequent.

In 1856, a wildfire swept over the Rancho San Julian, destroying most of the dry grass. A drought in 1857 further added to the cattlemen's woes. A letter from Joaquin de la Guerra at Simí warned that most of the Simí cattle would die unless moved to San Julian, but that was not possible on account of the fire and the need of the cattle for the green feed there. The letter stated that eight thousand to ten thousand cattle in Los Angeles County would probably die of starvation. And that was but a mild drought compared to the one yet to come.

The beginning of the end came for the de la Guerras when, on January 12, 1860, Gaspar Oreña sold to Francisco Antonio, Pablo Andrés, Miguel, and Antonio Maria the Rancho Espada, for which they agreed to pay $70,000 (with an initial payment of $15,000 and payments of $10,000 a year at 8 percent interest). Unable to make the second payment on May 29, 1861, the de la Guerras mortgaged their Simí and Las Posas ranches to Isaac Cook of Los Angeles for $25,000. These two ranches were worth perhaps ten times the value of La Espada, but the de la Guerras foolishly encumbered those valuable properties instead of taking their loss on the original payment on La Espada.

On October 16, 1861, unable to make the payments, they sold everything—San Julian, Simí, Las Posas, La Espada, and Conejo, together with the cattle—to Oreña for $150,000. Imagine José de la Guerra doing such a thing!

José de la Guerra died on February 11, 1858, at the ripe old age of seventy-nine. He was preceded in death by his wife, his sons Juan José and Raymundo, and daughters Rita de Jesús and Ana María de la Guerra Robinson.

However these circumstances came about, we see in José de la Guerra a man uniquely qualified to take full advantage of the opportunities unfolding before him in a frontier land rich in natural resources, lightly populated, and unexploited. In education, training, background, and influence, de la Guerra had few peers in California. His training in his uncle's commercial establishment, his schooling in accounting, his ambition and ability, his connection with Caracaba, who was *habilitado* of the Californias and secretary to the Viceroy, his friendship with Governor Arrillaga and his uncle's high post as secretary of the Spanish Army in Madrid, not to mention his growing influence and friendship with the padres of the mission, who named him their syndic—all combined to enhance his prestige and power as comandante of the Presidio of Santa Barbara. H.H. Bancroft wrote of him that "there was no other man in California who wielded such an influence for good as José de la Guerra."

De la Guerra's achievements in the political realm were modest, but might have been great had they not been constrained by his Spanish birth, which prevented his election as governor of California. Whether or not he would have been effective in politics is hard to judge, especially in view of his later reluctance to support his brother-in-law as governor when Carlos Carrillo, who had been appointed by the Mexican government, tried to claim the post but was thwarted by Alvarado and his more numerous *arribeños*.

De la Guerra's financial achievements can be considered as successful and perhaps, in modern view, spectacular, and he might be considered a tycoon by contemporary American standards. His commercial ventures by present standards were modest, yet consistently profitable, and he contributed goods to the economy of California that might not have been otherwise available.

But de la Guerra was unable to bequeath to his sons the most valuable of his assets, namely, his good sense, sound judgment, and erudition, which had stood him in such good stead. After his death we find his sons speculating in cattle during the drought and buying when they should have been selling and, at the same time, paying ridiculous prices for livestock in the face of imminent disaster. They lived the "life of Riley" without regard to their precarious financial circumstances, and mort-gaged all of their landholdings in order to maintain their life style, expecting to pay off the mortgages when times improved. Instead of getting better, times got worse, and by 1870 the de la Guerras, of course, had lost most of their landholdings at San Julian, Simí, Las Posas, La Espada, and Conejo.

To his sons Miguel, Pablo, José Antonio, and Francisco Antonio, de la Guerra bequeathed most of his real estate and the balance of his chattel after making gifts to some of his other children. The four sons were named by him as his executors, with full power to act in their capacity without bond.[65]

Bancroft wrote that the whole of de la Guerra's estate was squandered away so that within a year not an acre was left to the family. This is not strictly true, for they were ranching on San Julian and owning land and cattle until 1864, at least six years after his death.

The Sons and Daughters of José de la Guerra

OF ALL of the thirteen children of José de la Guerra and María Antonia Carrillo de la Guerra, the one who seemed to hold the most promise was Juan José, the fifth child and third son. After his schooling at Hartnell's School in Monterey, he was sent to college in England where he attended the Catholic college at Stonyhurst. But there he frittered away much of his time and was considered a "lady's man." He returned to California and went to Monterey, where he lived with his sister, María Angústias, and her husband Manuel Jimeno. There he died at an early age from a fall off a horse.

The one who achieved more prominence than any of the other sons was Pablo, who was the eighth child, after Ana María. Pablo Andrés was sent to a college in Mexico but, because of his Spanish citizenship, was not allowed to matriculate; he completed his college education in California. Pablo trained as a lawyer and spoke English fluently. He seems to have had a great deal of influence over the rest of his brothers, who deferred to him in the management of the ranches after the death of their father.

Pablo was a delegate to the 1849 State Constitutional Convention

Pablo Andrés de la Guerra

and later became a state senator and lieutenant governor. He was a champion of his race and did his best to see that his countrymen were given the treatment they deserved. He was considered to be a good legislator by his peers and a good, if not spectacular, orator.

When his term in the legislature expired, Pablo received a federal judicial appointment to the Fifth District Circuit Court and served ten years, resigning on account of ill health.

Sacramento was a dreary place to live, and Pablo often chided his wife, Josefa Moreno y Castro, for not writing to him. In one letter he told her that if she did not write to him he would take "an Indian mistress." Whether this threat had any salutary effect or not is unknown, but it is doubtful that she complied.

Pablo Andrés was a tall handsome man who seems to have been one of

Josefa Moreno y Castro de la Guerra

the few de la Guerra sons who was not spoiled as a young man. Miguel, also, was fairly capable. He, Pablo, José Antonio, and Francisco were named as executors of José's estate upon his death.

Pablo married Josefa Moreno y Castro, and the couple raised four children: Carlos, Francisca, Herminia, and Delfina. Carlos was married briefly until his wife ran off with another man. Francisca (''Quica'') married Thomas B. Dibblee. (My mother, Mercedes, was their daughter.) Herminia married Charles Lee, who died and left her widowed for many years. Delfina remained unmarried and lived in Casa de la Guerra in Santa Barbara until she moved away to live with a friend in 1943. The de la Guerra house had been sold around 1920 to Bernhard Hoffmann, who turned it and some adjoining property into the well-known Paseo de la Guerra.)

41

Miguel de la Guerra

Captain Antonio Maria de la Guerra

After José's death in 1858, Pablo and his family occupied the east wing of the Casa de la Guerra, and Miguel and his family the west wing, a part of which was sold to the antique dealer Falvy after Miguel's death.

Pablo Andrés de la Guerra died in 1874 and was buried at the foot of the altar in the Old Mission Santa Barbara, near his father and mother and his sister, Ana Maria Robinson.

During the American Civil War, Antonio María joined the United States Army and was commissioned a captain of cavalry. He departed Santa Barbara with a company of volunteers and rode off to the south-west, where some skirmishes with Southerners took place, but as for actual fighting, the company was not engaged. He had contracted one of the social diseases, then treated by the injection of mercury, but the cure was worse than the ailment and after his return he died a painful death when the mercury caused him to lose his lower jaw and teeth.

After the loss of their ranches, with no income or training for any particular career, several of José de la Guerra's sons turned to politics and public office and were variously engaged. One became mayor of Santa

Barbara, another a county clerk and recorder, and the others any job they could find. José Antonio and Francisco moved to Los Angeles. Francisco first married Asunción Sepúlveda and had two children; upon Asunción's death, Francisco married his sister-in-law, Concepción Sepúlveda, with whom he raised another ten children.

The first daughter of José and Maria Antonia, Rita de Jesús, did not marry.

Their second daughter, María Angústias, married Manuel Jimeno, who became Alvarado's lieutenant governor and often acted as governor when the latter was inebriated. They had eleven children, and Jimeno took

The sala (or parlor) of Casa de la Guerra in 1876. Seated on the left is Francisco de la Guerra. The lady in the center is his daughter, and on the right, Josefa Moreno y Castro de la Guerra, widow of Pablo de la Guerra.

Ana María de la Guerra Robinson,
wife of Alfred Robinson

three of his youngest sons to Mexico. María Angústias and her brother Pablo Andrés tried to bring them back, but to no avail. After Jimeno's death in Mexico, María Angústias married Dr. James Ord, a major in the U.S. Army who was later promoted to general. They lived in Washington, D.C., after the Civil War and became caught up in the whirl of society there. Angústias was a vivacious woman and a keen observer of the local scene, writing several short books of accounts of life in California of her time. She bore one child to General Ord, whom they named Rebecca.

Ana Maria married Alfred Robinson and went east to live out her life there. She bore Robinson six children: James, Elena, James Miguel, Anita, James II, and Alfred. We knew one, Elena, who married a man named Goodwin.

José and María Antonia's last child was María Antonia. She married Cesario Lataillade, the French consul in California. After his death by an accidental gunshot, which occurred when he was handling a gun, María married Gaspar Oreña.

Dibblees and Hollisters

OWN by the river in London there stands a stately mansion built around a large quadrangle. Somerset House was the palace of the Dukes of Somerset until one, as chancellor of the exchequer, absconded with a large sum of money. The Royal Family then appropriated the palace and lived there until forced by unsanitary conditions to abandon it.

It was to Somerset House that I was directed in 1955 to see the Great Register, that huge tome listing the inhabitants of the British Isles.

By a happy coincidence, since I knew the approximate dates of their departure from England, I was able to find the names of Robert and Thomas Dibblee (sometimes spelled Deeblee, Dibble, or Dible), who were listed as emigrants to America in 1635. They were named as "husbandmen" or cattle raisers, with the notation that the latter was a "soror." They departed Weymouth late in the year and arrived at Dorchester in the Massachusetts colony in 1636.

Herbert Eugene Bolton, in his history of New York's Duchess County, states that "the first Robert Deeblee, who, it seems, had been one of the founders of the church at Plymouth in England, arrived at Dorchester about 1633–34," but from my research in London, it seems he had departed Plymouth for the colonies in late 1635, arriving in Massachusetts in 1636. This is corroborated by Hoonton's *Emigrants to America,* found in the Round Room of the British Museum. It would seem then that this latter version is the more likely correct.

Bolton continues:

... [I]n 1637 [Dibblee] was elected a "freeman" of Massachusetts. He was named balif [*sic*] in 1637 and twice again in 1639, probably dying shortly thereafter. Robert's son, Thomas, meanwhile had arrived at Dorchester to join Wareham's church, and in December of that year, a grant was made to him which amounted to about thirty acres, which was granted to both father and son. Thomas was elected a "freeman" of Massachusetts in 1637 and moved to Windsor, Massachusetts, the same year. He raised a large family there, one of whom, Ebeneezer, married Mary Wakefield and was killed in December 1675, during King Philip's War at Narragansett. He died insolvent, leaving several children, besides his widow. One of these children, Wakefield Dibblee, after the death of his first wife, married Jane Fyler and later moved to Danbury, Connecticut, where he became a member of the State Legislature. He died in 1734, just about 100 years after his great grandfather had arrived in America. Wakefield Dibblee's youngest son, Ebeneezer, became the first member of the Dibblee family to become well known outside of his community. He was one of the ultra-Tory members of the clergy in Connecticut. He attended Yale and graduated from that college with a Doctorate in Divinity and was among the dissenters [Congregationalists], but later converted to Anglicism and returned to England to receive his Holy Orders.

As a staunch Tory who had sworn fealty to King and Church, Ebeneezer feared the coming revolution that, if successful, would rend the church and make his position precarious, both politically and fiscally. This proved only too true when, to the great resentment of his parishioners, he continued to support the king from the pulpit. Funds from the Mother Church had dried up, as the Church of England refused to support a congregation of rebels. Ebeneezer's fiscal problems became acute, and he wrote: "I must end my days in want, dishonor, and contempt."

Admittedly, Ebeneezer Dibblee was not tactful in his dealings with his neighbors, and resentment against the Dibblees grew so violent that most of the rest of the Dibblees left the colonies for Canada, where still they ran into hard times. But Ebeneezer managed to hang on and gradually mellowed. He was eventually awarded an honorary doctorate by Columbia University in 1793. He died of cancer of the lip in 1799.

Ebeneezer's son, also named Ebeneezer, moved to Pine Plains in New York, near the Hudson, where he purchased some land and married a Miss Harvey. Their son Fyler married Frances Wilson, a daughter of William Wilson. Wilson's brother, Sir Alexander Wilson, was a doctor knighted for bringing Princess Victoria into the world. William Wilson emigrated to America and settled in Livingston Manor, New York, in 1784.

Fyler Dibblee served as an artillery major during the War of 1812 and became a judge in Duchess County, later moving to New York City, where he became an alderman and served as president of the Jackson Marine Insurance Company. Fyler and Frances Wilson Dibblee raised four sons and one daughter: Albert, Thomas, Nellie, William, and Henry. Fyler's untimely death prompted his eldest son, Albert, to enter a clearing house in order to support his mother and four siblings. Albert seems to have been spectacularly successful, for besides financing Thomas's education at Columbia and supporting his mother and sister, he purchased for his brother William a seat on the New York Stock Exchange. Albert acquired some land along the Hudson, near Poughkeepsie, where he raised fine merino sheep. His farm was adjacent to that of Samuel F.B. Morse, the inventor of the telegraph.

Shortly after the first Dibblees came to America, John Hollister landed on those same shores, probably about 1640, and settled in the Connecticut Colony, where he joined the local militia. He and his son, John, received some fairly large grants of land from the King of England.[1] In those days, land grants were laid out in straight strips, mainly headed westward, and John Hollister and his son each received a grant. The son joined the local church, but for some unknown reason was excommunicated by the pastor. The senior Hollister, however, rallied his fellow parishioners around him, and the pastor was expelled and Hollister reinstated. His father returned to England. The junior John Hollister then joined the local militia and attained the rank of lieutenant.

The Hollisters prospered in their new lands, but sold all their Connecticut lands in 1806 and bought a large farm in Ohio.[2] John Hollister married Philena Hubbard, and to them were born several children, the eldest of whom was named William Welles Hollister. There was a sister named Lucy and a younger brother, Hubbard.

William attended nearby Kenyon College, where his interests in agriculture, animal husbandry, and horticulture were nurtured.[3] He returned home before graduation, on account of his father's death, and managed the increasingly prosperous farm, in which he was particularly successful. William Hollister was considered to be one of the most successful farmers of the region.

The Move West

In 1848, Albert Dibblee was seriously injured on a New York City street by a falling bale of hay that knocked him to the ground. His doctor prescribed a long rest, preferably a sea voyage, for the injured man.[4]

Albert arranged the purchase of a small vessel, a brig, that he stocked with tools and merchandise, and set sail for California in late 1848. Arriving in San Francisco, he found the city in ruins and smouldering from its latest gold-fever conflagration. He did find a ready market for his cargo. But because of the glut of vessels for sale, Albert was unable to sell the brig as he had planned. Sailors, upon arrival in port, deserted the ships for the inland gold mines, so there were many crewless ships waiting for a buyer. A great number of these vessels rotted and sank in the shallow bay, only to be covered later by the land fills that reached out into the water to make more land.

Albert formed a partnership with a man named Chichester, but that unfortunate fellow soon died of the plague. He again formed a partnership, with a man named Crosby, and together they engaged in the lucrative business of buying goods on the East Coast and shipping them to San Francisco. Large amounts of coal were among the items shipped.

Albert Dibblee formed another association with the Comstock

shipping interests of New York, owners of the clipper ships, and thus augmented the flow of merchandise, which was in ever-increasing demand. Gold was the medium of exchange in California, while goods purchased on the East Coast were paid in currency. Thus, a tidy profit of 15 to 20 percent was realized on the exchange rate on top of the markup on the merchandise sold. Gold was shipped to New York and exchanged for dollars, which were then used to purchase more goods for shipment.

The risk of shipping gold, however, was considerable, as Albert learned to his dismay. A vessel carrying one of their shipments sank and the gold, which was supposed to have been insured by his partner in New York, was lost. The partner, it seems, had been taking the risk by pocketing the premiums and, when the loss occurred, was unable to pay.

Another difficulty was the instability of the banking system and the frequency in which banks became insolvent. But his early bank training enabled Albert to monitor a bank's assets so that he never got caught in a bank that failed.

From his association with the banking community, Albert learned the value of credit and financial responsibility, and it was not long before he put these to good use.

In 1858, Albert Dibblee purchased, partly on credit and partly in partnership with William Corbitt, the 15,600-acre Santa Anita Ranch near Arcadia,[5] which had been granted provisionally by Juan Alvarado to the Scotsman, Hugo Reid. The grant to Reid was later confirmed by Pio Pico in 1845.

Albert and Corbitt commenced to raise sheep and plant the ranch with fruit and vineyards. Needing someone to manage the property, Albert asked his brother William to join him in the venture, but William was otherwise occupied, so Albert prevailed upon Thomas, who was practicing law with the firm of Stuyvesant Fish & Sons in New York, to make the move. Thomas arrived in California in 1860, by way of Cape Horn, and immediately assumed management of the ranch, settling boundary disputes and supervising the planting of orchards and vineyards. Thomas received an undivided quarter interest in the ranch. He planned to have his mother and sisters come out, but that never happened.

William Welles Hollister   Joseph Wright Cooper

The horticultural endeavor was unsuccessful and soon abandoned, probably due to the lack of fencing that allowed deer and rodents to eat the trees and vines. But the sheep venture was a great success. Their flocks multiplied and were improved by the importation of purebred Rambouillet rams from Vermont. Albert and Corbitt were soon selling breeding stock throughout California and as far away as Texas.

The quality of native sheep in the American southwest had improved little since Spanish rule ended in 1821.[6] The unofficial policy of the Spanish government discouraged the breeding of high-quality sheep whose wool might compete with that of Spain.

In 1851, while Albert Dibblee was becoming established in San Francisco, the young Joseph Cooper of Missouri joined a sheep drive headed by a Colonel Peters. Traveling westward along the banks of the North Platte River and into Wyoming, they had started the trek too late to make the crossing of the Sierras before winter set in, and the sheep drive was halted at Devil's Gate on the Sweetwater River. Leaving the sheep and some of the men behind, most of the party, including Joseph Cooper and his brother-in-law Hiram Pipes, proceeded on to California. They reached the gold fields and started mining, but their luck played out and the two men turned to teaming, transporting goods to and from

Stockton along the Mariposa River. This venture brought good returns, so when they had saved enough money for their passage home, they left San Francisco by boat and crossed the isthmus at Panama, partly on foot and partly in canoes paddled by Indians. Fortunately, they did not contract the yellow fever prevalent in the region.

By the time they arrived back in Missouri, where they found conditions still depressed, Cooper and Pipes decided to return overland to the California goldfields with another group of men. Cooper, having traveled the route before, was chosen leader of the group. They were fortunate in being able to avoid an ambush by Indians in Utah. Again, they tried their luck at mining, and again they were unsuccessful, so Cooper and Pipes resumed the teaming and hauling of supplies from Stockton and Sacramento to the mines.

The story of Joseph Cooper's several trips to the coast is told by Frank Sands in his book *A Pastoral Prince*, from which these accounts of his odysseys were taken.

In the meantime, according to Walker Tompkins, William Welles Hollister, farming in Ohio, caught the gold bug and, in 1851, joined a contingent of men crossing the plains to El Dorado. The men were in such a hurry that they took many dangerous chances in crossing swollen streams and rivers when, with only a few days' wait, the danger would have been abated. But it seems they were afraid that the gold would disappear from the California hills ere they reached the promised lands. Hollister deprecated their haste and diminished the hardships of their crossing in an interview with H.H. Bancroft fifteen years later, perhaps when the trials of the trip had grown dim in his memory, for hardships there surely were.

Hollister reached the mines but was not impressed with the rowdy surroundings. He sold his horse and bought passage on a river steamer down to San Francisco. The disorderly city likewise caused an unfavorable impression on Hollister, and he determined to return home by steamer. Unable to book passage for a month, he rented a horse and rode south to Monterey County.

Spring had come and gone and the California landscape was dry, as occurs every year. As Hollister rode along the rolling hills of San Benito County, he saw large flocks of poor-quality sheep that looked fat and healthy despite the lack of green grass. His curiosity aroused, he sat on the ground (according to Walker Tompkins) and tried to determine the source of the nutrients that nourished these sheep to such an extent. He decided the nutrition lay in the tiny clover seeds entwined in the clover burr, and he pondered long on this discovery.

Miles upon miles of these rolling, clover-covered hillsides stretched along the landscape—hillsides upon which thousands of sheep could be pastured. The climate was salubrious, water was within easy reach, and land and labor were cheap (herders received perhaps five dollars a month).

Fired with enthusiasm, Hollister returned to San Francisco to convince fellow emigrants to join in his venture, but they laughed at him. How could sheep be brought across the plains with all of the hostile Indians? Besides, it was too far to make such a drive. Hollister finally was able to book passage home by way of the isthmus at Panama. His enthusiasm undiminished, he began making plans for the sale of the family farm in Ohio.

With the consent of his brother Hubbard and financial assistance from his sister Lucy (who had inherited a small fortune from her late husband), Hollister assembled four thousand sheep, drovers, cattle, horses and wagons, and all manner of appurtenances, including a portable forge, extra irons for the tires, jerky, beans, flour, sugar, coffee, and all of the staples and pots and pans necessary for the two-thousand-mile voyage. They had no illusions regarding the hardships they would encounter— hostile Indians, storms, drought, fire, and river crossings—but Lucy was indomitable and as determined as William to make the grade. She drove the wagon, tended the horses, cooked for the men, nursed the sick, and was ever-ready to defend against hostile Indians with her Remington repeater rifle.

A long delay in assembling the sheep and equipment set them back nearly two months, so it was not until July that the expedition left St. Joseph, Missouri, for California. They were not lacking in well-wishers, for the whole town turned out to cheer them off, several accompanying them on their first leg out.

Progress was slow but steady, and the two dozen men (and Lucy) performed their tasks with precision as the cattle were driven along behind the wagons. Game became more abundant, so they had plenty of meat; there was little trouble with Indians. They followed the route used by Colonel Peters, along the North Platte River, until it was decided that instead of going the northern route, which would likely be covered with snow, they headed toward the Salt Lake and the California desert.

After entering the Nevada desert, their severest trials began, as good water was scarce and several days without water passed before they reached the Virgin River. There they encountered another sheep drive, headed by two Bixby brothers and a man named Flint, also headed for California. According to Walker Tompkins, the sheep refused to cross the river and had to be carried. This seems a bit ludicrous since there were about eight thousand sheep in the two flocks.

The threatening Mojave Desert lay just ahead. Some of the drovers wanted to turn back, but were persuaded by Hollister, and the promise of a bonus, to continue on. The crossing of the desert just after Christmas took its toll. Of Hollister's original four thousand sheep, only one thousand reached the San Bernardino Mountains and water a week later.

The two flocks rested there a few days before Hollister proceeded up the coast; the Flint-Bixby contingent stayed in the south a while longer. Incredibly, of the twelve million acres of land in California, the Flint-Bixbys and Hollister both chose the same land to settle on: Francisco Pacheco's San Justo Ranch in San Benito County. The price was higher than either could pay, so they agreed to divide the land.

Albert Dibblee had established a reputation in San Francisco as an honorable and good businessman who knew the ways of high finance. He realized the need for explosives in the mines, so he established the Giant Powder Company to manufacture dynamite.[7] He corresponded with Alfred Nobel,[8] the inventor of dynamite, and was soon doing a booming business as the major supplier of that commodity.

Because of the dangers involved, shippers from the East were loath to send dynamite that far by ship. Albert offered his brother Thomas shares in the company, a profitable concern.

Among his other activities, Albert became one of the largest wool merchants on the West Coast, and soon came into contact with William Hollister and the Flints, who had arrived at the San Justo Ranch.[9]

Joseph Cooper had returned to Missouri, but for him the lure of California still was strong, and he decided to make another trip.[10] Circumstances again brought him into contact with Colonel Peters, who was planning another sheep drive with Hubbard Hollister; the two agreed to take on Cooper as a partner in the venture.

The flocks were assembled from April through June, 1860, and the expedition set out in early July. There were, besides twelve thousand sheep, one hundred head of cattle and twenty-five horses and mules, all tended by twenty-two men, including the owners. This was Cooper's third westward crossing and it was destined to be his longest and the most difficult.

Missouri, Kansas, and New Mexico presented few problems as feed was abundant and the weather temperate. When they reached Arizona, winter had set in, and, because of the scarcity of feed and trouble with their hooves, the condition of the sheep deteriorated. This was one of the most troublesome problems encountered in all of the great sheep drives and seems to have contributed more to the delays and losses than any other factor.

Wear from the abrasion of rocks and sand contributed to the soreness of the sheep's feet. Puncture wounds in the flesh between the cleft of the hooves (caused by the points of burned-over grass and sharp-pointed seeds) exacerbated the sheep's sore feet, as did the caked clay from around the water holes that dried in the clefts of the hooves. After all this, the animals were unable to travel great distances and their conditions became poor or they died.

As the warlike reputation of the Apaches was well known, the party approached New Mexico and Arizona territories with some trepidation. The Indian agent at recently abandoned (1859) Fort Thorn, a Dr. Spock from Pennsylvania, was on good terms with the Apaches and arranged a feast to which twelve of the chiefs were invited to meet the newcomers. All went well, and it was agreed that the party could remain unmolested in Apache territory until proceeding on.

The month was January, and lambing was due to start soon. In February, eight thousand lambs were born to augment the original twelve thousand sheep. Winter—and perhaps the Apaches—took a huge toll in both sheep and lambs. By the time the party reached California, there were fewer than five thousand animals in the herd. Fifteen thousand animals had been lost, and there is no explanation as to how or why this happened. It seems likely that the wily Apaches, aware that nothing could be done to stop them, simply absconded with most of the sheep.

When it was planned to rest the flock in Arizona, sixteen of the men decided to press on to California. They were given eight pack animals to complete their voyage. Meanwhile, Colonel Peters returned on business to his home in the Midwest. Mexican herders were hired to replace the men who had left for California.

The sheep were shorn in mid-summer, and the proceeds from the sale of wool were used to pay the expenses of the operation. In September, with Peters' return, the drive resumed. They had been in Arizona for eight months, and it was time to continue on to California before the advent of winter.

Their greatest trials occurred in the crossing of the great desert around the Gila River: forty hours with very little feed and no water. They found ample feed and good water when they reached the river at Gila Bend. Proceeding downriver, they crossed the Colorado at Yuma, entering Mexican territory and traveling westward until near San Diego County, where they crossed again into California.

In San Diego County they found abundant feed, so progress slowed to allow the sheep to recuperate. Near San Luis Rey, they camped for the night beside a small lake. As it started to rain, a nervousness prevailed among the sheep for a short while, and then a flash of light filled the air and seemed to linger around the bodies of the sheep. Their mouths, ears, and hair assumed an eerie glow that gradually faded away to a luminescence outlining their bodies and lasting a minute or two. This might have been marsh gas ignited by lightning (recorded in English literature as "the marsh's meteor lamp,") or perhaps static electricity, familiar to mariners as St. Elmo's fire. Whatever the cause of the phenomenon, it left the men and animals thoroughly frightened and bewildered.

During the journey, none of the men had been seriously ill or injured. There were no serious fights, and no one was killed along the way. An incident occurred in the early part of the trip that points to the compassionate side of Joseph Cooper's character:

While passing through Oklahoma territory, the party met a young Mexican boy, who told them that a band of desperados had taken his horse from him. Cooper and the boy went back to the desperado's camp to persuade the men to release the animal to the lad, but the men threatened Cooper and the lad with bodily harm if they persisted, so they departed. In the evening the boy stole back into the camp and retrieved his horse and joined the drive for a few days to throw the men off his trail. Then he was off to Mexico, waving a grateful farewell to his benefactors.

After allowing their sheep to rest and recuperate for a few weeks in San Diego County, Colonel Peters separated his flock and proceeded up the coast, where he found pasture on the Zaca Ranch. Cooper and Hubbard Hollister moved their sheep up to the San Fernando Valley. Cooper was preparing to return to Missouri for a visit when they received word of Peters's death and a proposal to sell his flock.[11]

Hollister and Cooper journeyed to Zaca to attend the sale, and there met the Dibblees and William Hollister, all of whom had planned on buying some of Peters's sheep. These were good Merinos, a grade of sheep hard to come by in the West. Each bought some of Peters's sheep to augment their own increasing flocks.

With the new sheep safely joined with his own flock, Cooper returned to his home in Missouri in the late fall of 1862.[12]

Relations between William Welles Hollister and the Flint-Bixbys became strained despite the latter's willingness to trade with Hollister for their land in San Benito County, which contained a greater proportion of flat land.[13] The trade was proposed by Hollister, who, in his prophetic way, saw possibilities in subdividing some of the land into lots and establishing a town, which would be named Hollister and result in huge profits to him.

Despite his continued desire to acquire an interest in Tecolotito Ranch near Winchester Canyon in Santa Barbara, Hollister remained in San Francisco, for a young lady had stolen his heart. According to Walker Tompkins, the lovely Hannah James was nearly twenty years Hollister's junior; Hollister was considered one of the most eligible bachelors in town, and he apparently had made his mark on the fair Jenny (as Hannah was called). Their engagement was announced in early June 1862.

The death of rancher Nicolás A. Den had put a crimp in Hollister's plan for the acquisition of the Tecolotito Ranch. In the interim he purchased the Cholame Ranch in San Luis Obispo County, postponing the day for the purchase of his dream land. Hollister never did things in a small way. He was accustomed to spending money on a grand scale. Most of the money to finance his high living was lent to him by his sister, Lucy, who was never repaid.

The drought of 1862–64 forced the Dibblees to seek pasture for their sheep.[14] Their foreman, George Long, reported that there was feed in Santa Barbara County, so they leased a ranch on the banks of the Ventura River in 1862. Hubbard Hollister and Joseph Cooper were also looking for feed for the sheep they had brought out. Their flocks had wintered the season of 1862–63 in the San Fernando Valley while Cooper visited Ohio. Hubbard Hollister wrote that "the San Fernando Valley was a hellish place to raise sheep on account of the Devil Winds." These winds dried up the small amount of moisture that fell there during the state's worst of all recorded droughts—a drought that was to bring such unthought-of consequences to the economy and livelihood of many of the old inhabitants, all of which were staggering beyond imagination. It is very likely that no one had ever contemplated the possibility of such a catastrophe disrupting their lives and reducing most landowners to bankruptcy and worse. To some it meant their very existence. For some newcomers to the state, and for many who had waited long and patiently to acquire land, the drought was a long-awaited opportunity.

To William Hollister, Joesph Cooper, and Albert and Thomas Dibblee, the chance of a lifetime came when they discovered that there was a fair amount of feed on a Lompoc ranch they were soon to acquire.

The Lompoc Valley

The 38,335-acre Rancho Lompoc had been granted by Governor Juan Alvarado in 1837 to Joaquin and José Antonio Carrillo just a week after the San Julian had been granted to José de la Guerra. Their brother, Anastasio Carrillo, had received a grant to the Punta de la Concepción, just to the south, in May of the same year. The Carrillo brothers took possession of their Lompoc ranch in 1839 and grazed cattle there for several years, thereafter renting the land to John Foster, who grazed nearly seven thousand head of cattle on the place for several years.[15]

On the north Rancho Lompoc was bordered by Rancho Jesús María of José Valenzuela, and on the east by Santa Rita and Purísima of Ramón Malo. To the southeast was Cañada de Salsipuedes, which had been granted to Pedro Cordero but was later acquired by John Keyes.

The Carrillos, like many of their contemporaries, encumbered their Lompoc holdings with a mortgage to T. Wallace More and his brother in 1855. Anastasio Carrillo mortgaged a part of his coastal ranch, Punta de la Concepción, to Charles Fernald and the balance later to Gaspar Oreña. Fernald and Oreña took possession in 1859.[16]

Unable to satisfy the terms of the mortgage on their Lompoc ranch, the Carrillo brothers deeded the place to Henry and T. Wallace More and R.M. Turner in June 1862.

William and Hubbard Hollister, Joseph Cooper, and the Dibblees arranged to lease the Lompoc ranch.[17] Light rains and a lack of cattle had allowed feed to grow there. The following year the lessees paid More's asking price of $60,000 for the sale of the property. The Dibblees took a mortgage for their one-third share; William Hollister took another third and lent Cooper and Hubbard money for their third.[18]

Shortly after their purchase of the Lompoc ranch, a long and costly boundary dispute ensued between the partners and Lewis Burton, who had received the adjacent Jesús María Ranch from Valenzuela, and with

W. Ap Jones, who laid claim to certain lands in Lompoc north of the river. (Jones had married Ramón Malo's daugher, Ramona.) The suit dragged on for eight years while lawyers for both sides shuttled back and forth between California and Washington, where the case was being heard before the U.S. Land Commission.[19] Finally, a compromise was reached with Burton, to the dismay of Albert Dibblee, who felt that their case against Burton was nearly won. But Jones was not disposed to compromise. Eventually, a *diseño* was found in the land office in Washington proving that the grant to Purísima was a *sobrant*, and the Lompoc partners won their case against Jones.

The matter settled, a U.S. patent was issued to the new owners in November of 1873, just about ten years after their purchase of the land.

These boundary disputes were a common occurrence in California for several decades following the American occupation and appear to have been caused by the slipshod methods used by the Spanish and Mexican authorities in surveying and describing the land grants. It is evident from accounts of these surveys and from the descriptions of the boundary lines that the surveying instruments used to measure angles and direction and the chain used to measure distances were seldom if ever used, although such instruments were in use in the American colonies at least as early as the eighteenth century.

The reason for this is unclear, but probably arose from several factors. The first was a philosophical attitude of the governing bodies during the early period. Because of the large and virtually limitless expanses of land, and the few people desiring to occupy those lands, rather casual re-cording methods resulted. This eventually created a chaos of land disputes on a scale seldom seen in modern history.

Another factor may have been the lack of expertise among the citizens. A perusal of the curricula at Loyola College in Los Angeles reveals an absence of courses in almost all of the sciences, such as engineering, botany, chemistry, astronomy, physics, and even medicine. Since these were church-run institutions, it seems that the church's position discouraging the dissemination of scientific knowledge was a dominating factor. Possibly the lack of qualified teachers among the clergy brought about the same results.

In many cases concerning land boundaries, the distances described between certain points were so far from accurate as to cause Sherman Day,[20] the surveyor general of California at the time, to state that:

> [I]n this case [the Lompoc description], they undoubtedly went on the land and went through the form of stretching a cord in the distance of the lines and then guessed the distances. They say that all of the Spanish measures are found incorrect and, as a rule, are far short of the actual distances between natural points.

In describing the course as proceeding from a well-known landmark in some (usually vague) direction, such as northerly or northwesterly, for approximately so many *varas* or leagues to some other described landmark, the length of the cord could vary with the changes in temperature or humidity. It was virtually impossible to follow a straight line between two points without the aid of an instrument, resulting in overlapping on noncontiguous boundaries. Rivers and streams often changed their courses over the years, and described trees and even boulders would sometimes succumb to the ravages of time and the elements and disappear, so that the location of these boundaries, once thought to be well-defined, often became, in time, vague and conjectural or even nonexistent.

The price the partners paid for much of this Lompoc land and later purchases amounted to about $1.25 an acre. A San Francisco paper of the day criticized these men as "dolts" for paying such a high price for the land, while more recent critics have referred to their purchases as a "land grab."[21]

Complaints from wool buyers in the East about burrs in the wool caused concern among the partners in Lompoc and they soon learned that the scourge of sheepmen throughout the Southwest had infected the Lompoc lands in the form of cockleburs and Mexican thistles, seeds that were spread rapidly by the sheep from the weeds' natural habitat along the river over much of the Lompoc plain. These burrs have curved tentacles on the seed pod and are extremely difficult to remove from the wool.

Determined to remain in the sheep business and spurred on by

Hollister's success in establishing a settlement on his San Justo Ranch in northern California, the partners let it be known in late 1871 that, once their titles became secure and a patent had been issued, they were planning to subdivide their Lompoc Valley lands into farm lots and establish a town near the upper end of the valley.

A civil engineer named Bennet was hired to survey and subdivide the lands in early 1874. It was decided that the two main streets of the town should be wide enough so that a wagon drawn by a team of six horses could turn around in the middle of the block in each. The valley was divided into farm lots of various sizes in order to accommodate the needs of a variety of prospective landowners.

A land company was formed, with the partners subscribing a specified amount of money to operate the venture. The selling price of the land was determined at $500,000, with payments stretching out for an indefinite period of time. What with depressions and droughts, which often caused a delay in payments, this period turned out to be nearly three-quarters of a century, so that the Dibblees owned land that had not been sold as late as the 1940's.

Joseph Cooper and Hubbard Hollister, meanwhile, decided to pull out of the Lompoc partnership and purchase the adjacent 15,523-acre Rancho Santa Rosa in the Santa Ynez Valley from the widow of Francisco Cota. His generous offer was immediately accepted by the owner, and W.W. Hollister again came to their rescue by lending his brother and Cooper money to make the purchase. Hubbard's early death in 1873 placed a heavy burden on Cooper to finance the venture and pay back W.W.

The sale of the Lompoc lands started auspiciously enough to make the partners feel that they had made a good deal, but as time went by, depression again enveloped the economy. Among their other troubles, one of the partners, Hollister's brother-in-law Phineas Banning, feeling that the money would be slow in coming, refused to sign the deeds of sale. According to letters he wrote to Thomas, Albert Dibblee had to resort to harsh measures to induce Banning to sign.[22]

W.W. Hollister and the Dibblee brothers then formed a partnership

Thomas Bloodgood Dibblee

Francisca "Quica" de la Guerra Dibblee

in which each of the three would hold an undivided one-third interest in any further purchases of land and sheep; from the sale of his San Justo holdings, Hollister would lend the Dibblees money to start the purchase of adjacent lands on which to pasture their sheep.

They had leased the San Julian and La Espada ranches from Gaspar Oreña, who had acquired these ranches by mortgage from Anastasio Carrillo in 1852.[23] The purchase of San Julian was contingent on the partners also purchasing La Espada, which stretched along the coast to Point Arguello. This was not entirely to the Dibblees' liking, since it was not as good grazing land. As money from Hollister's sale of his northern ranch came pouring in, the surrounding ranches of Salsipuedes, Santa Anita, Gaviota and, later, Las Cruces were added to the domain, containing over 125,000 acres. These lands were all purchased by Thomas Dibblee in his name; undivided one-third interests were then deeded to Hollister and Albert Dibblee.

"Punta del Castillo" (left), the magnificent home of Thomas B. and Francisca de la Guerra Dibblee, can be seen at the right in the above photograph of the beach at Santa Barbara looking southwest, taken about 1887. Castle Rock is at the far left. Designed by architect Peter J. Barber and built on an imposing site overlooking the city, the house was a prominent landmark for several decades until it was destroyed in the earthquake of 1925.

Once their land acquisitions were complete, Hollister turned his attention to his many other affairs, leaving the matter of organizing the huge sheep operation in the capable hands of his partners: Albert Dibblee in San Francisco, who was the banker and financial expert, and Thomas Dibblee, who had moved to Santa Barbara (to marry Francisca de la Guerra) and was to oversee the details of the huge enterprise and attend to the legal end of the business. It was a winning combination, this partnership, with each of the three men having implicit faith in each of the others. It is questionable if there was any other successful sheep operation of such size in the whole state of California.

An operation of such magnitude needed an exceptionally competent sheep man, and it is doubtful that, without the services of George Long, their operation could have been such a success.

Born in Lancaster County, Pennsylvania, in 1815 of "Pennsylvania Dutch" stock, George Long was engaged in the mining and manufacturing business in that state. He came to California in 1852, made a small fortune in gold mining, then returned to Pennsylvania. Like many before and after him, Long succumbed to the lure of the Golden State and returned again to the mines, this time unsuccessfully. After drifting around for a while, he found employment on the Dibblees' and Corbitt's Santa Anita Ranch as their sheep superintendent. It was Long's experience, together with great industry and good judgment, that prompted the Dibblees to make him general superintendent of the sheep operations that they and Hollister had begun in Lompoc and had expanded into a ranching empire. Long oversaw the construction of the large system of corrals, chutes, dips, and barns (designed with the aid of Rufus T. Buell), which enabled the large business to operate like clockwork. The logistical problem of handling such huge numbers of sheep (at one time forty-five thousand head) was tremendously complicated. Herds from Salsipuedes, Jalama, Santa Anita, Las Cruces, and San Julian[24] came in orderly fashion to the headquarters to be sheared and dipped, and the timing of the arrival and corralling of the bands was a feat worthy of an army strategist.

Eventually, a combination of factors (including the competition and lower prices of wool from New Zealand and Australia and the introduction of foxtail and ripgut brome) favored a change away from sheep raising to cattle. As the number of cattle gradually increased, we find that between 1885 and 1887 their numbers had grown from 1,571 to 2,761.

But sheep continued to be an important factor. Records show that in March 1893, thirteen years after the division with Hollister in 1880, there were still six thousand sheep on San Julian.[25] A small band of sheep remained on San Julian until the middle 1920's and on Cooper's adjacent La Vina ranch until the death of William Cooper, Sr., in the late 1940's, when his son took over the management of the ranch.

Purebred shorthorn bulls were purchased in Canada, and good quality cows of the same breed were obtained from the Chowchilla Ranch in the San Joaquin Valley. That ranch later came into the possession of the Lansdale and Howard families. (Theodore Howard, son of Agnes Poett Howard, married Olivia Lansdale.)

Nicolás A. Den and his brother, Dr. R.S. Den, who had both owned ranches in Goleta, were sorely pressed for money. However, according to historian Walker Tompkins, after they sold their property to Hollister, the Dens "resumed their extravagant style of living,"[26] and, with little income, were quickly depleting their capital. In 1879 they "started casting about to see how they could replenish their coffers." This reached the ears of Thomas B. Bishop, who was practicing law in San Francisco. Bishop determined that a strong case could be brought against Hollister over the land he had purchased from the Dens without court approval, and that very likely he would be willing to come up with more money for the land. Hollister considered this blackmail and refused. He continued to pour money into the property on the theory that the more he put into the place, the more secure it would be.

A suit was filed in superior court, and Hollister won on the first round, but the Dens appealed, and the verdict was against Hollister on all counts; his financial difficulties, with high court and attorney fees, started to mount.

A depression had set in and the prices of wool and mutton had fallen to such an extent that the partners were reluctant to sell their wool.

Albert Dibblee had assisted Colonel W.W. Hollister in his financial affairs for years, acting as adviser, agent, and de facto banker for the Colonel, and in keeping his accounts. He went so far as to choose a diamond ring from Shreves when the Colonel requested.

Hollister's financial difficulties had prompted Albert to summon his brother Thomas to San Francisco for a conference. It was decided that the brothers should terminate their partnership with Hollister lest his possible brankruptcy drag them under.

A following chronology of events leading to the climax of Hollister's troubles shows his precarious legal and financial situation.

Colonel Hollister's Troubles

The first indication of financial difficulties came on September 9, 1879, when Albert wrote to Thomas:

> W.W. is in trouble with bank. He paid off note to Low with $50,000 borrowed from bank. Bank of California refused further credit.
>
> P.S. I hate to be involved in Col's. affairs for years to come. I see nothing but trouble of the worst kind. He is terribly frightened. If we buy him out, it should be mostly cash, or perhaps three-fifths cash and two-fifths note payable after spring clip.

In the next letter, dated September 20, 1879, Albert discussed the possibility of buying out Hollister with Hollister's right to repurchase within four to six months. On November 18, 1879, Albert wrote:

> Bad news. Stow says has private knowledge that W.W.'s appeal will be against him. Keep news private. Best come to S.F. for a final accounting. Danger that someone will attach partnership account if unable to collect from W.W.

On November 20, 1879, Albert wrote: "W.W. sold his interest in Lompoc to Adams for $50,000."

November 21, 1879: "Broom has notified W.W. that suit for $5,000 will begin November 28 unless he is paid before that date. His business looks alarming."

Thomas returned to Santa Barbara and found Hollister sick in bed. The Colonel readily signed the document Thomas presented to him, in which a division of the properties was made. Hollister's wife objected to the transaction, but Hollister had complete confidence in his partners and told his wife that they would never take unfair advantage of him. She was unmollified and in later years complained bitterly that her husband had gotten the worst of the deal: "They took the pie and left us the crust."

The next letter from Albert stated that "Col. reserved the right to come back as joint owner with the Dibblees." Follows another letter, of November 29, 1879:

"W.W. received word that the Arlington [the famous hotel which Hollister was building at the time] would be attached unless he sent check by return mail."

December 16, 1879: "[Supreme Court] Decision against Hollister on all points. Looks fearful. Appears no hope for him or [Ellwood] Cooper. W.W. in today."

A year later, December 12, 1880: "Advise buy W.W.'s interest in sheep at price, terms and conditions you suggest, with his right to repurchase."

The physical division of the properties into nearly equal portions, as initially approved by Hollister, included in Hollister's portion the coastal ranch, La Espada, as well as Jalama and Salsipuedes, while the Dibblees would get San Julian and the Gaviota Ranch to Arroyo Hondo.

Hollister, with no particular attachment to the land, as had the Dibblees with their connection to the de la Guerras and San Julian, agreed to the brothers' proposal. Later, Hollister decided that he would rather have the coastal strip in the event the railroad came through, as it would be more readily saleable, and the Dibblees agreed, so Hollister traded that portion for Jalama.

Immediately after the division, the Dibblees mortgaged their holdings for $50,000 in order to repay Hollister the money he had loaned to them.

Hollister's share of the sheep had been attached by the banks, but he was later able to lift the attachment. A meeting was arranged between the Dibblees, Hollister's attorney Stow, and Bishop to see if a compromise could be worked out. It was pointed out to Bishop that Hollister controlled the rights to the water from the forest land, and that he could cut it off at will. It was stated that two of the Den boys living in San Francisco were without funds and would very likely sell their share of the ranch. But negotiations came to naught.

It was while these events were transpiring that there was again trouble with the sale of the Lompoc lands because of Banning's refusal to sign the deeds of sale, on the grounds that the price was too low. Albert finally induced Banning to sign the deeds.

The sale and liquidation of many of his assets enabled Hollister to extricate himself from some of his difficulties, and he thus averted the loss of the Arlington Hotel, although the heavy expenses of the suit continued.

Comfortably settled in their mansion on his Glen Annie estate, Hollister's attention turned to the Arlington Hotel.[27] Upon completion, "the social whirl of Santa Barbara revolved about him and his wife, who entertained lavishly, as befitting Santa Barbara's leading citizen. . . ." Their civic contributions were virtually boundless and Hollister reveled "in the role of the social lion," according to Walker Tompkins.

But Hollister was increasingly worried by the thought that his beloved Glen Annie would be lost to him. The preoccupation and worry gradually wore him down and he finally succumbed to an illness on August 8, 1886.

Tompkins has written that Hollister's predominating ailment was dropsy, probably accentuated by acute edema from a failing liver and kidneys.

Hollister had led an exciting and eventful life filled with adventure and accomplishments. Not one to flinch from a challenge or fail in support of a worthy cause, he was considered a dreamer by some of his acquaintances. But he was a practical man of many and varied interests. Compassionate of his fellow man, he drove himself hard when the occasion demanded. His many accomplishments and civic endeavors mark Hollister as one of the empire builders of the nineteenth century. Had he chosen politics as a way of life, there is little doubt that this man, with so much drive and foresight, might have attained high political office. He was indomitable.

When the Hollister saga eventually emerges, as it surely will some day, there will stand revealed possibly a great man of many talents and tremendous abilities.

The case before the Supreme Court was finally decided against Hollister, and a sheriff's notice of eviction was served against the widow. The very night that they vacated the great mansion on Glen Annie, a mysterious fire of unknown origin burned the house to the ground.

The irony of this case was that the Dens received a pittance for their share of the property, with the lawyers taking the lion's share, including most of the land. All of those years spent and enemies gained—to what purpose? True, the Dens regained from Ellwood Cooper the land across the road, which seemed to have little value, except that Mrs. Bell believed what a geologist had told her, that oil would be found under the land. The Bells and the Lutons hung onto that piece of land at all cost, to be amply rewarded when, in the middle 1920's, great gushers of oil were discovered by the Rio Grande and Barnsdall oil companies, resulting in millions of dollars in royalties to the landowners.

Albert and Thomas Dibblee died in December 1895, within weeks of each other, both having put their affairs in order after the division of their properties in the early 1890s. Thomas's estate was left in trust, with the widow inheriting the Casa San Julian and about four thousand acres; the balance went to his children to be divided when the youngest, Delfina, reached the age of thirty-five. Albert Dibblee had lived in California for forty-six years, Thomas for thirty-five years. Each had contributed a good measure to the growth and progress of the state. Albert's voluminous letters were carefully kept; those kept in Marin County fortunately not destroyed by the San Francisco earthquake and fire of April 1906. After Albert's death, his correspondence was given to Harvard University, but after the death of the donor (Albert's son Benjamin Dibblee), Harvard returned them to California, where they now repose in the Bancroft Library at the University of California in Berkeley. The Dibblee Letters, together with the de la Guerra Archives at the library in Mission Santa Barbara, span nearly the whole of the nineteenth century and are treasure troves for future historians.

Judge Ogden Hoffman, Jr.

The Land Act of 1851

THE LAND ACT of 1851 was so important and of such great concern to the landholders of California that a review of the act and the debate in the United States Senate regarding this bill and its passage through the courts, as reported by the *Congressional Globe*, seems appropriate.

The Treaty of Guadalupe Hildalgo ended the state of hostilities between the United States and Mexico on February 2, 1848. By the terms of that treaty, Mexico was forced to cede to the United States Texas, California, and the territory of New Mexico (comprising the future states of New Mexico, Arizona, Colorado, Nevada, and Utah).

For this territory, the United States agreed to pay to Mexico the sum of $15 million and to respect certain provisions proposed by the Mexican government, among which was a proviso that the U.S. would respect Spanish and Mexican land grants made up until the time of the American occupation in 1848.

The great influx of immigrants into California that followed the discovery of gold in 1848 brought irresistable pressure upon U.S. legislators to open more land to settlement by new immigrants, some of whom viewed the large landholdings of the old settlers as an injustice to "the rights of the conquerors."

The Land Act was introduced into the United States Senate by Senator William McKendree Gwin of California in January 1851. This bill was viewed by many in and out of Congress as confiscatory and in contravention of the treaty.

The Senate, in considering the bill, presumed without so stating that most California land titles were invalid, and imposed certain rigorous conditions requiring the landholders of the state to prove the validity of their titles. The bill required every grantholder to appear before a board of commissioners in California to present his claim, and, if an appeal was desired from any decision of that board, whether by the landholder or the government, then appearance should be made before the Federal District Court of Appeals. If either party appealed that decision, evidence and arguments were to be submitted before the Supreme Court of the United States.

At each point in these proceedings, the landholder could be challenged by any number of third parties who might have claims, however spurious, to his land.

Many of the old settlers (who had held their land for ten, twenty, or thirty or more years) spoke no English. Some were uninformed about the legal proceedings, and in some cases, without the necessary funds to hire lawyers. Thus they found themselves challenged to prove the legality of their claims. The landholder would have to pay for representation in San Francisco as well, except for one session to be held in the south.

Senator William Hart Benton of Missouri (father-in-law to Col. John C. Frémont, a large landholder with a Mexican grant) was one of the most vigorous opponents of the bill. He declared: "It was confiscatory and gave contestants the power to attack a landholding without having a legitimate claim." Benton further stated that many of the claims were spurious and nothing less than harassment.

Senator Gwin replied that "there were very few perfect titles in California and none of the grants had been surveyed." He stressed the need of a survey in order to perfect a land title and proposed an amendment requiring the issuance of a patent.

Senator Benton then proposed an amendment to that amendment that would "recognize the rights of prescription in favor of possessory rights as applied to individuals," and stated that "even the shortest time of rightful possession is an index of title, which is good against the world until a perfect title is made out." He went on:

> [I]n all countries which have laws, time, under certain limitations, becomes a title and a perfect title, against which nothing can prevail. The civil law of prescription is fair, equitable and beautiful, more perfect in its three degrees of thirty, twenty, and ten years than any of our statutes of limitations.

Benton averred that, "under common law, long possession without any evidence whatsoever is full title," and "in every state of the Union there are statutes of limitation, only varying in time, under which possession is a title in itself."

The debate rose to a high plane when a Senator Underwood quoted Roman law and the Code of Justinian to prove that the civil law of prescription applied only to individuals and not to individuals vis-a-vis the government.

Senator Dawson referred to Bayard Taylor's *El Dorado* as authority:

> [T]he only grants which are legal and which convey good title under the existing laws of Mexico must come under the two acts, those of 1824 and 1828, and . . . in no case can a governor make grants of any land lying within ten leagues [about thirty miles] of the coast, or within thirty leagues of the boundaries of any foreign power.

The authenticity of these statements is questionable.

Senator Henry Clay said that "the treaty is sufficient and the settlers' rights should not be enlarged," while another senator raised the spectre of Catholicism rampant in California. He said that Benton's amendment would allow the missions to lay claim to huge amounts of land, to which Senator Pierre Soulé of Louisiana pointed out that "the missions had been secularized and owned no land whatever." He went on to state that the attitude was one of "Voe Victus—Let the conquered beware, they must be crushed."

Senator Benton proposed that the board of commissioners should meet in every county in which land claims had to be adjudicated and that the board should be a board of only preliminary inquiry. His motion was defeated.

Benton objected to specifying an actual date for the take-over by the state, citing the action of the Senate in refusing to do so in ratifying the Treaty of Guadalupe Hidalgo.

The reason for the Senate's inaction was the "McNamarra Affair," in which a British subject, McNamarra, residing in Mexico City for over a year was involved in a deal whereby Mexico, in a last-ditch attempt to thwart the occupation of California by the Americans, would grant to McNamarra some three thousand leagues of land (approximately thirteen million acres) in the eastern San Joaquin Valley. As negotiations concluded about the middle of 1846, it was planned that McNamarra would be transported from Mexico to California aboard a British man-of-war as a show of force by the British (who had their eyes on the state and were not acting wholly without prejudice). McNamarra would then be invested with the land (contrary to Mexican law, since only Mexican citizens could be granted land by the Mexican government), while British seapower stood by to prevent any interference with the plan (presumably by the Americans). However, a flaw developed when John C. Frémont by land, and Robert Stockton by sea, appeared on the scene with sufficient force to dissuade the British from carrying out their scheme.

The Land Act passed the Senate with neither Benton's nor Soulé's amendments and went to the House, where it passed without discussion, and was signed by President Millard Fillmore.

With the passage of the Land Act of 1851, it became incumbent upon President Fillmore to appoint a commission and a judge to preside over the court of appeals. The appointment of a judge was of considerable importance, since his decisions would likely tilt the balance either in favor of or against the interests of those seeking a liberal interpretation of the bill.

In setting up an appeals court, President Fillmore did not, as was customary, consult with the senior senator from the state, since he and

Gwin were at odds politically. He consulted Secretary of State Daniel Webster as to the appointment of a judge to fill the post. Webster recommended the son of his good friend, Ogden Hoffman, a senator from New York. Young Ogden Hoffman had recently graduated from Harvard Law School and had established law offices in San Francisco. Despite some misgivings as to his youth and inexperience, the appointment was ratified by the Senate and Ogden Hoffman became the focal point for most of the important decisions affecting the land disputes in California.

As decisions by the U.S. Court of Appeals and the U.S. Supreme Court proceeded, it became evident that much of Senator Benton's philosophy regarding the landholder's rights was being upheld by the courts' decisions. One held that "a description of a land grant, aided by a *diseño*, was held sufficient." Another read: "The rule of common law that the construction of deeds quantity must yield to the specific metes and bounds, cannot be applied to Mexican grants." It appears that the court was saying here that a survey of metes and bounds was not essential in all cases, and it went on to state in another case that "an actual survey was not necessary to all boundary lines, where some of them can be determined from old lines or natural boundaries." And again, echoing Benton's plea for the recognition of possessory rights, the court ruled "an inchoate title founded by juridical possession presents an equity which the United States is bound to respect."

These two cases undoubtedly had a bearing on the settlement of the Las Cruces case. The court found in favor of Miguel Cordero's heirs, despite the fact they had neither filed nor presented their claim before the Land Commission within the prescribed time, and that the land had been declared government land open to settlement. It destroyed Gwin's contention that "an inchoate title cannot be the basis for a deed."

Even the absence of an actual grant was, in some cases, "excused" by the court, where it was proved to the satisfaction of the court that

[W]here the governor intended to accede to a position, and the land had been occupied and enjoyed under the grant, or the promise of a grant, and by everybody recognized as belonging to the grantee, the latter has an equitable title which the United States will respect. [U.S. v *Soto*, case 16357]

Finally, the court decreed that "the patent issued upon a confirmed Mexican land grant is the final, authentic, and conclusive record against persons having no title." (*More* v *Foster*, case 9784.) Judge Hoffman further ruled that a land grant made under Spanish or Mexican rule was valid if the governor, or *auyentamiento*, had made a grant (following a request for land) if the territorial deputation had approved the action. This approval was generally given after a determination had been made as to whether the conditions of the grant had been met. (Such conditions might require that a grantee should build a house and live there within one year. Other conditions were also imposed in certain cases, such as the construction of a mill, or that a certain amount of land be cultivated or planted to orchards, or that the land be stocked with cattle, sheep, or horses.)

In the case of de la Guerra's grants to Conejo in 1822 and San Julian in 1837, it appears that he was excused from certain conditions (*i.e.*, that he reside on the property), because his duties kept him at the presidio.

Although a preponderance of the cases favored the landholders, the effects of the litigation were destined to plague most of the old settlers for nearly a generation, by reason of mortgages or heavy borrowing, to contest the actions. While the bill did not immediately accomplish the objective of breaking up the very large landholdings (the owners of many of those ranchos, such as the Carrillos, Vallejos, Yorbas, Stearns, Sepúlvedas, and de la Guerras, were better able to finance the costly legal proceedings through mortgages and borrowing), it did set the stage for the eventual loss of most of these holdings, because the landholders were rendered financially vulnerable, and most were unable to recover from the terrible drought of 1862–64. While the change in the system was inevitable and mourned by many, it is possible that its occurrence at an early date, and through peaceful means, may have prevented more serious problems; the pressure of a rapidly increasing population demanded more land. Indeed, the newcomers were, on the whole, more interested in agriculture than in large-scale cattle raising, and this more intensive use of the land was deemed necessary to satisfy their needs for more food and fiber and to furnish homesites. It is doubtful if the old-time ranchers would—or could—have adapted themselves psychologically to this type of activity, which required much more labor than to which they were accustomed.

Henry Dibblee

ENRY DIBBLEE, Albert's and Thomas's youngest brother, had come west by way of Panama and trekked to Salt Lake City. There he observed and disapproved of the Mormon's practice of polygamy. He continued on to Red Bluff in the Sacramento Valley, near the California gold fields, where in 1871 he established a retail store. It was not long after that he started speculating in wool, lost all of his money, and had to be bailed out by Albert Dibblee.

Before that time, however, he had succumbed to the wiles of a young lady and had asked her to marry him, to which she agreed. One day, in the barbershop, a new man in town asked Henry if he had heard the news that Henry Dibblee's girl had run off with another fellow. This, I think, put an end forever to Henry's hope of marriage. He remained a bachelor the rest of his life.

After his bailout by Albert, wherein he agreed to come to San Julian and help the partners run their large operation, Henry left Red Bluff for the ranch, arriving at San Julian sometime in early June 1875. Henry's first impression of the ranch, as noted in two letters to his brother Thomas, extoll the virtues of the arrangements on the ranch, including the modern plumbing and bathing facilities. He approved of the chimneys in the men's bunk houses, which would obviously help prevent fires from the charcoal or kerosene heaters. He marvelled at the extent of the hospitality shown by the partners in welcoming so many people for free meals. He wrote to Thomas:

If you want to do a hotel business here, probably no difficulty would occur in obtaining customers. Although you are steadily taxed with lodging and meals for travelers, given gratuitously, it of course is one of those incidental matters that you desire should be cheerfully met. . . . Doubtless many a kind word is thereby spoken by them for you and [Superintendent George] Long far and near.

It is, however, curious to see how the travel continues at any hour of the day both ways. People are so well treated, they almost intuitively stop here on their way to Lompoc to take a meal and rest themselves and horses.

The first evening I came there were two or three people who stopped but a short time at the gate, a couple later taking supper.

Next afternoon, Mr. Smith and daughter put up with wagon and horses for the night Friday, Col. Hollister staid [sic] here and left with Mr. Long next morning for Lompoc. [Hollister was then a partner.] Saturday about one p.m., three men, Messrs. Farling, Steele and some other name, stopped with their teams, took dinner and left for Lompoc. Yesterday [Sunday] morning Mr. Casebear with his daughter Rose and his son stopped for a short time and I think took breakfast with Mr. Long.

I have not seen anyone yet this morning. I suppose the best way to view this is that it affords good facilities at all times for good communication with [Santa Barbara] and enhances the estimate of your Rancho in the view of the community at large.

This gracious practice, alas, lasted well into the twentieth century, when the cook would invite all and sundry to come for lunch or dinner. It got so bad that all of the trades people and many others, including the riders' children, would be there for breakfast. That is when Bill Dibblee and I, after Wilson Dibblee's death, decided to close the kitchen and have the workers board themselves. Too much money had gone down the drain over the century that the men's kitchen was in operation, and it

Henry Dibblee at Casa San Julian, ca. 1900.

was time to stop such waste. Being a good neighbor was one thing, but being a sucker was another, and one which I could not abide. "*La grande mano*," as quoted by cousin Eduardo Koch, no longer could be tolerated.

Henry Dibblee kept the ranch accounts and saw to the ordering of groceries, etc., and his presence helped to keep nepotism, whereby brothers or sons of the workmen were given favored treatment, from creeping into the system.

A large parcel of land, called Tract A, had been set aside for the benefit of Henry Dibblee, but so frugal was he that he never needed more than his salary. His greatest preoccupation was reading, and his extensive library of the classics is an example of the good taste in which he indulged.

Uncle Henry Dibblee died in 1910, having spent thirty-five years, about half of his life, on San Julian. Almost every day, year in and year out, Uncle Henry wrote to his brothers about the activities on the ranch. He alone could measure the rain in the old rain-gauge. Not much missed his keen eye, and he knew who loitered and who worked. Although his penmanship in later years leaves something to be desired, his accurate account of the goings and comings on the ranch and the records of rainfall, cattle branded, or sheep sheared provide infallible details of the activities of San Julian. Henry Dibblee was a short man, but his words carried a lot of authority over me, as he would point his finger at me and say, "Don't you swing on that gate," referring to the wooden gate in front of the Casa, and I can almost hear him to this day, seventy-nine years later, with his admonition.

The Poetts

ALFRED POETT, my grandfather, was born in Concepción, Chile, in 1839, the youngest of three children. His parents, Dr. Joseph Henry Poett of Dublin and Sarah Wood Poett, were married after he went down to London to set up a medical practice.

Immediately after their marriage, the couple was informed that they would be forever exiled from England. Sarah Susanna had been a Ward in Chancery before her marriage and the circumstances surrounding this fact caused their exile.

The couple went to live in the Azores, where there was a fairly good-sized colony of Britons living there for their health. The colony welcomed the presence of a British doctor (although he was reputed to have gone around in the early mornings breaking the windows of some of his patients so that they would get fresh air to cure their tuberculosis).

The couple moved to Chile, where they lived at Concepción.

In 1848, Sarah Susanna died; the following year, Dr. Poett married the Scottish Mary Michael. The family set sail for San Francisco, where they arrived shortly after one of the many conflagrations that would virtually destroy the city in the nineteenth century.

Living in San Francisco were two friends, one of whom, William D. Merry Howard (a successful merchant), had recently lost his young wife.

Howard's friend was John Redington. The two young men went down to the docks to see incoming vessels, as was their custom, for there were usually interesting things to buy or new people to meet. When the gang plank was lowered, the two young men gallantly escorted Dr. Poett's two beautiful daughters off the boat.

When they were out of earshot of the young ladies, Howard said to Redington, "I am going to marry that beautiful young lady."

"And I am going to marry her equally beautiful sister," replied Redington.

It was love at first sight and their prophesies came true, for Howard married Agnes Poett and Redington married Julia, and they became the focus of the Howard and Redington family of San Mateo and Santa Barbara.

For several years, Agnes remained without child, until she went one day to a legendary spring to partake of its miracle waters and lo! she soon became pregnant. William Howard died, however, and she married his brother George, by whom she had several children.

In San Francisco, Dr. Joseph Poett set up a tent hospital and administered to the sick and injured.

He sent his son, Alfred, back to England for his college education. Alfred did not attend the University of Dublin, as had his father and grandfather (the latter had served as major in the medical corps of the Bengal Lancers in India).

At Greenwood College in England, Alfred matriculated in civil engineering and went to Glasgow to apprentice with George Martin for his vocation. In 1858 he departed England for the Azores, where he surveyed the rail line from Lisbon to Oporto. He returned to London and obtained employment under the well-known civil engineer Fred Turner, who supervised the layout of the Metropolitan Underground railway system in London.

In 1863, Alfred Poett went by ship to San Francisco, where he found employment as an engineer with the newly arrived Central Railroad. He was commissioned to survey a line from San Jose to Watsonville for the railroad.

Alfred Poett

Mary Louise Williams Poett

He was employed by Senator Leland Stanford to lay out the grounds of his large estate at Menlo Park. On this estate, Stanford had laid out a racetrack. It happened that Stanford and Collis P. Huntington became involved in a wager of $25,000 as to whether or not a galloping horse has all four feet off the ground at one time. Stanford insisted that it was so and Huntington took the opposite position. Living in San Francisco at the time was William Muybridge, who had come from England and had done pioneering photography in Yosemite. Stanford engaged Muybridge to determine by means of photography who was right. Muybridge set up an ingenious way in which the cameras set around the track would be tripped by the galloping horse, and it proved conclusively that it was as Stanford had supposed. Muybridge took many photographs of humans walking; his photographs appear to have been a forerunner of the moving picture. Alfred, a friend of Muybridge, undoubtedly witnessed the event, for he was presented with a series of slides showing the horses in motion.

Alfred served as a surveyor for the War Department in Arizona, New Mexico, and California. He was chief engineer for the Fresno River Canal and San Joaquin irrigation districts and surveyed for the Mexico railroad to Mazatlán. He was engineer for the Mazatlán waterworks and a variety of other projects.

Alfred Poett did a considerable amount of surveying for the banker Ralston and presented him with a bill for his services, whereupon Ralston told Poett to pick out a piece of property that suited him from Ralston's large San Mateo holdings. The transaction was verbal, and when Ralston supposedly committed suicide by walking into the bay, Alfred Poett was left without any proof of the agreement, unable to collect for his services.

In October 1891, Alfred Poett was engaged by Albert and Thomas Dibblee to do a survey of their 48,000-acre Rancho San Julian. He started the job immediately and worked at it for over four and a half years.

Alfred Redington Poett

Toward the end of 1894, Albert Dibblee was ailing and his mind became less clear. He grew impatient with the delay in completing the survey, despite his brother Thomas's efforts to explain the necessity of completing what had been started. Albert complained that the ranch was generating too little revenue and he did not want to incur further expenses; Thomas persisted in seeing that the survey was completed.

Alfred Poett's compensation for his services as surveyor amounted to $10 a day, with food supplied by the owners. His first assistant received compensation of $2.00 a day; a second assistant, his son Alfred R. Poett, was paid $1.00 a day.

Bill from Alfred Poett to Thomas and Albert Dibblee for
surveying Rancho San Julian in 1893-94.

Alfred Poett surveyed in Santa Barbara County, and his maps are demonstrations of his accuracy and professionalism.

Alfred Poett married Mary Louise Williams, a young Philadelphian whose father, Dr. Henry B. Williams, was a brother to Edward Williams, a partner in the Baldwin Locomotive Works. Mr. and Mrs. Poett lived in Hillsborough, where they had built a house.

Mary Louise Poett was seriously injured in a San Francisco streetcar accident. The couple came to Santa Barbara, but she died as a result of the accident, and Alfred Poett continued to live in his cottage on the 300 block of East Mission Street in Santa Barbara, where he owned two lots, each with a house. He died there in 1910 at the age of seventy-three. The two-story house in which we lived was later torn down and the lumber brought to Yridises on San Julian, where we built a house in 1919.

Alfred Redington Poett, my father, was the third of Alfred and Mary Poett's four children (Henry W., Marion, Alfred R., and Mabel). When the elder Alfred Poett came to survey San Julian, his son often came to work for him on the chain gang (at one dollar a day). While at San Julian, my father met Mercedes, daughter of Thomas Dibblee and Francisca de la Guerra. They were married in 1902.

Efforts to Buy
and Sell San Julian

SPORADIC efforts to sell and offers to buy San Julian began in August 1883, when a man named Louis Tomasini of Petaluma offered $500,000 for the property. Nothing ever came of the proposal, for reasons unknown.

The next effort to sell the ranch came in the late 1880s, when Harrison Gray Otis of the *Los Angeles Times*[1] printed a rosy brochure extolling the virtues of the ranch and its large profits, which were slightly inflated. He wrote that it would be possible to subdivide the ranch into dairy farms, and proposed that a price of $30 per acre would be paid for the land. It had been anticipated that the Southern Pacific Railroad—and a boom in land values—would soon be coming down the coast.

Albert Dibblee had subscribed $50,000 to a rival line, the Atlantic & Pacific Railway, which was to be a subsidiary of the Santa Fe Railroad. Albert expected to become a director of the line, which had come into Los Angeles in 1882, provided it would be able to gain first rights-of-way to San Francisco. Albert, contemptuous of the rival Southern Pacific, called it "Stanford's Sham," and wrote uncomplimentary letters to Thomas regarding Leland Stanford, Collis P. Huntington, Charles Crocker, and Darius O. Mills—the Big Four. He characterized Huntington as "one of the slipperiest men imaginable" and said that the "railroad is just laying back in order to obtain more money for subscriptions [of right-of-way]." When it appeared that the Southern Pacific was making progress down the coast, the Dibblees attempted to get the line to run through San Julian. A survey determined that the grade was steeper than the 1 percent the railroad engineers deemed appropriate, so the S.P. took the coastal route instead.

During the twenty-year interregnum before the line was completed between San Francisco and Santa Barbara, the Dibblees hired an engineer named Judson to submit a preliminary survey between their wharf at Gaviota and Lompoc, but his report discouraged the partners on account of the large numbers of trestles that would have to be constructed along the coastal route. Albert later wrote to Thomas advising him not to invest in Ellwood Cooper's scheme to "bridge the gap" between Santa Barbara and Paso Robles because, he said, "Ellwood Cooper is so far removed from the world of high finance that his plan is bound to fail." Nothing ever came of the idea to raise $15 million to construct the line.

The Dibblees had set aside for the benefit of Henry Dibblee a tract of land on the east boundary of San Julian, known as Tract A, consisting of some 4,500 acres. After his death in 1910, these lands were sold to pay off the $75,000 mortgage Albert and Thomas Dibblee had incurred.

The next sale occurred in 1935, when the Santa Anita Slopes on the southern boundary of the rancho were sold in order to pay the inheritance tax assessed against the estate of our grandmother, Francisca de la Guerra Dibblee, who died in 1932.

In the mid-1930s, Wilson Dibblee often invited his good friend, the artist Edward Borein, to join us during spring roundups. One year Borein asked Wilson if he might bring a guest—Will Rogers. After his visit, Rogers sent a message through Borein asking if the family would entertain an offer to sell the ranch. After considerable discussion, it was agreed to hear his offer and to take a vote on the matter. It was agreed

T. Wilson Dibblee, 1933

beforehand that if but one person objected to the offer or did not want to sell, the offer would be turned down.

Borein came up and made Rogers's offer for the ranch, "lock, stock and barrel." The offer was for $1 million; my mother and Wilson Dibblee opposed the sale. Rogers eventually bought a ranch near Lompoc, the Jesus-Maria, which he gave to his son Jimmy. It was not long before the army took over the land to comprise Camp Cooke, which later became Vandenberg Air Force Base.

Other portions of San Julian have been sold over the years so that the 24,000 acres left by Thomas Dibblee now amount to a little more than 13,000 acres, not all of which is contiguous.

The Albert Dibblee heirs started selling their Jalama ranch in 1910. Within the next ten years they had disposed of most of their land. A portion of their Lompoc lands, however, remained unsold until the late 1930s, due to a dispute with the heirs of W. Ap Jones, who had owned a part of the Santa Rita. The river had changed its course and had eroded a portion of the land owned by his estate, and Jones claimed an acreage that encroached on a piece owned by the Dibblees. Finally, another man bought the two properties, which settled the matter.

Thomas Dibblee's estate was administered by three trustees: Charles Edwards and Henry Lincoln, both bankers from Santa Barbara, and his son-in-law, William T. Summers, who had married Francisca ("Pan-chita") Dibblee. Wilson Dibblee took over the management in 1910 and continued in that capacity until his death in 1951, at which time the ranch was again administered by a triumvirate. In 1969, our aunts all agreed to form a trust, and I was named manager, a position I have held since. At that juncture, it was decided to sell all of the cattle and lease the land—a hard decision after having raised livestock on San Julian for more than one hundred and thirty years.

Rancho San Julian:
Into the
20th Century

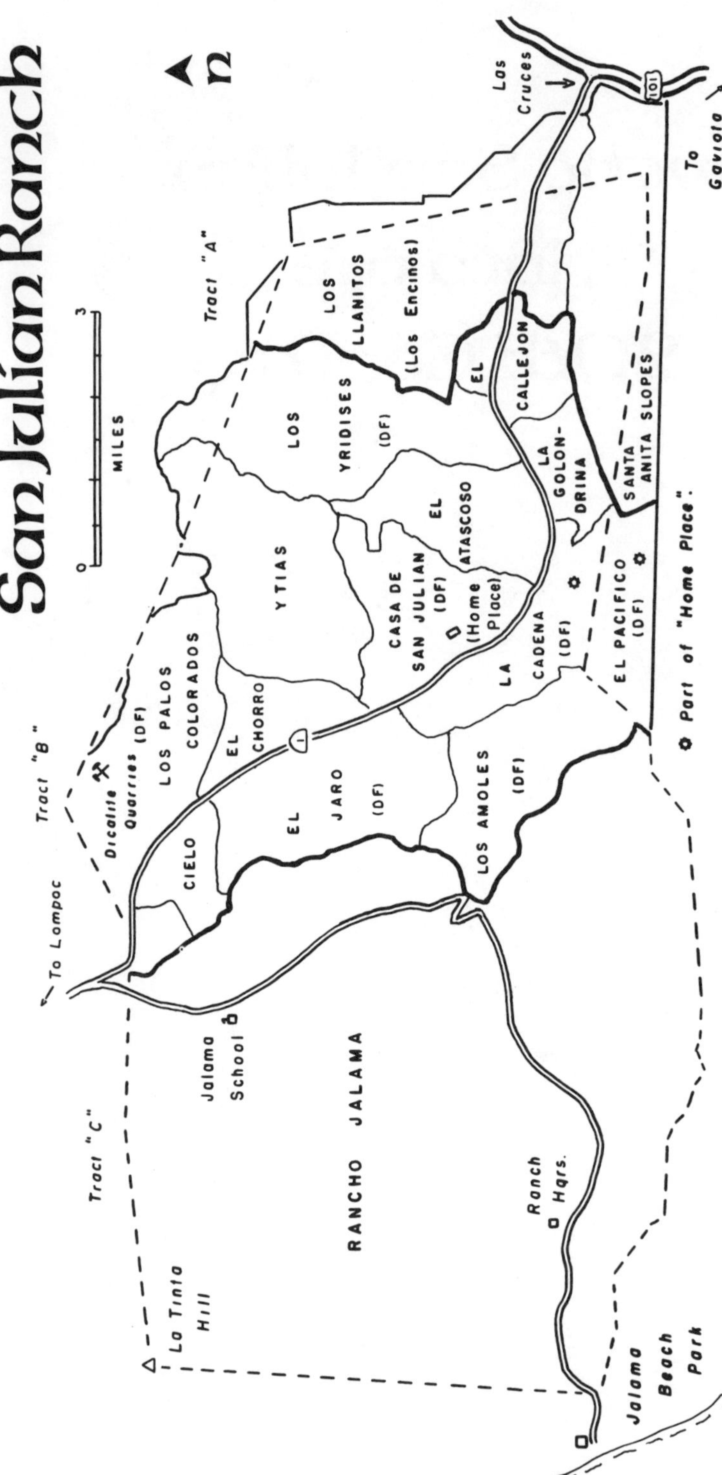

When the partnership of Albert and Thomas Dibblee and W.W. Hollister ended in November 1882, the Dibblee brothers eventually became the sole owners of the San Julian Ranch. The ranch was divided into three tracts as of April 1, 1892. Albert acquired the most westerly portion (Tract C), which later became the Jalama Ranch. Thomas received the center section (Tract B). The eastern section (Tract A) was held for Henry Dibblee, who declined to acquire ownership. Ownership of Tract A reverted to the estates of Albert and Thomas Dibblee and, beginning in 1913, various parcels were sold to outside interests. The boundary lines of the original San Julian grant (dotted lines) have been changed by subsequent sales and purchases as indicated by solid lines. Division of Tract B, in the Estate of Thomas B. Dibblee, was made in 1918 with segments of San Julian going to his descendants, including his daughter, Mercedes, the wife of Alfred R. Poett. Today, ownership of most of the ranches is still held in the names of various members of the Dibblee and Poett families.

Rancho San Julian

THE BOUNDARY of San Julian, as originally granted, crossed Las Nutrias Canyon, about a half-mile from the one-time hamlet of Las Cruces, where the present Highway 101 and the San Julian Road (State Highway No. 1) intersect in the Gaviota Pass. The line crossed the canyon and turned abruptly northward on the easterly side of the canyon up a steeply wooded ridge, past a lagoon near the top of that ridge, and along the western boundary of Miguel Cordero's Rancho Las Cruces.

The Corderos lived on land granted to them in 1836 by Governor Mariano Chico. In their splendid isolaton, they were unaware of, or unprepared to cope with, the terms of the Land Act of 1851. Their land was eventually declared to be public domain and, as such, open to settlement.[1] By that time, Miguel Cordero had died, and as time passed, undivided interests in his estate were sold by some of his children. Purchasers of those undivided interests included Miguel de la Guerra, William Welles Hollister, Joseph Cooper, and Albert and Thomas Dibblee.

When Las Cruces ranch was declared public domain, the Dibblees, Cooper, and Hollister joined the heirs of Miguel Cordero to oppose such action. Depositions were taken from neighbors attesting to the fact that the Corderos had lived on the land for over thirty years and that there was indeed a grant to the land (*diseño*). After a long search of the land office files, a grant to the land was found. An act of Congress in 1886 was required to issue a patent to the Corderos, who had occupied the land until them.

The northern San Julian boundary came to a *portesuelo* (swale) where Los Llanitos and Las Nutrias canyons meet on the ridge overlooking the Santa Ynez Valley, near where the boundaries of San Julian, Las Cruces, and the Rancho Santa Rosa of Francisco Cota were supposed to meet. But a government survey determined that there was a discrepancy in the original descriptions and that the borders did not come together. The Dibblees immediately filed on, and obtained title to, this long and sometimes narrow strip of land extending about four and a quarter miles along the top of the escarpment ridge and down the canyon to the westerly border of Rancho Santa Rosa in the Santa Ynez Valley.

Joseph Cooper retained a piece of the property surrounding the Cotas' old adobe.

In the early 1920's, the Dibblees, in order to settle some long-standing debts, decided to sell the portion north of Palos Colorados and adjacent to Cooper's Santa Rosa ranch, which we had named La Vina. Joseph Cooper's son, William, had started a promising walnut orchard, and he was desirous of acquiring the land. William Cooper deemed our asking price too high, and Gaston Dreyfus, a bean and real estate broker from Lompoc, met our price and acquired the property. Whereupon Cooper, fearing that he would lose a chance to obtain the fine land, purchased the property from Dreyfus (who made a nice profit).

Farther to the west was another one of those pesky parcels of land outside our boundary fence lines comprising some forty acres of land on a brushy hilltop. This land belongs to the Casa San Julian tract, but is not connected to it—Las Ytias of Francisca Dibblee Summers lies between the two properties. In 1926, it was decided to fence this rectangular piece, and so a crew of men and a wagonload of material were sent way up there to do the job. When hot weather intervened to ripen the corn crop, which had to be ensiled, the crew was called back to headquarters. One thing followed another, so that the fencing was postponed indefinitely. When we took over the operation of Los Yridises in 1932, after a disagreement on ranch management policy, I would visit the site when I went to check on our troughs nearby and look over our boundary fence with Tommy Donovan, our neighbor to the north. On one of these occasions, I was unable to find the sled that had contained the several hundred posts and rolls and rolls of barbed wire. Many years later, I was told that a neighbor had gone up there with a team and dragged the sled, with perhaps a thousand dollars worth of fencing, down the hill to his place.

That fellow was once accused by a neighbor of stealing a cow or steer from him. The brand inspector, Clyde Crowell, was called and the two went over to the neighboring ranch, where the accuser pointed out the animal to Crowell. When he examined the brand on the beast, it turned out to be a fairly new brand, but that of the accused rancher. So nothing could be done until the animal was killed. Several years passed, and the animal was sent to market, and Crowell, remembering the accusation against the fellow, went to the market and procured the hide, which indeed showed the accuser's original brand from the inside. What happened to the thief I do not remember, but we forever after gave him a wide berth.

Continuing the northern boundary line to the west, where Los Palos Colorados now meets La Vina of the Coopers and beyond at the Salsipuedes, the boundary turned quite abruptly southwestward and followed a straight line down the hills adjoining the Hollisters' Salsipuedes to the confluence of the San Julian and Jalama creeks. There it made a slight bend to the west and followed a straight line along the foothills of the lower Jalama Valley and up those hills to a point next to Anastasio Carrillo's La Espada, then on to the high hills we called La Tinta, which is south of Lompoc and where the tanbark oaks grow. There the boundary made a right-angle turn to the south and followed a straight line, passing east of Mount Tranquillon, the inactive volcano that erupted some twenty million years ago and left its evidence of volcanic tuft, phosphate, and bentonite (or volcanic ash) dispersed for many miles around.

On toward the ocean near Jalama Beach went the line, coming within a quarter-mile of the ocean, and then turning abruptly eastward and following the zigzag ridge of the earthquake fault for about five miles back toward Las Cruces. After leaving the vicinity of the ocean, the line bordered Rancho El Cojo and then came to another corner, where the San Julian, El Cojo, and Nuestra Señora Del Refugio meet, on a ridge where tall tanbark oaks abound. There the line turned northeastward for about a mile and then due east. It was found by survey that the boundaries of San Julian and Nuestra Señora Del Refugio did not meet, and several thousand acres lay between the two ranches. These were filed on by the Dibblees and Hollister, and when the separation of the two ranches was effected before Hollister's death, the land became Dibblee property. El Pacífico, named in honor of the squatter Pacífico Ortega, still remains in our possession.

Casa San Julian

CASA SAN JULIAN, or rather a portion of the west wing of the house, appears to have been built over an older foundation of what may have been a hut or very small shelter. Legend has it this hut was constructed by a priest and a soldier who often passed that way going from Santa Barbara to Mission La Purísima Vieja in the Lompoc Valley, perhaps as early as the late 1700's

When José de la Guerra was granted the San Julian lands in 1837, he was obligated to build a house on the ranch. He chose the location for the Casa near a stream flowing out of the hills to the north. The structure he built consisted of two rooms: a bedroom and a *sala* (living room), which probably was used as a dining room as well. The present kitchen and bathroom and a bedroom facing to the east were added later and are of wood construction.

The large kitchen adjacent to the *sala* in this wing of the house was used for nearly a century to prepare meals for the workmen on the ranch. The *sala* was used as their dining room for many years; its adobe walls are nearly two feet thick. The kitchen and two bedrooms adjacent and to the east, together with another dining room and a bedroom, constitute the second portion of the house built by de la Guerra's sons, who often came to San Julian for long periods to oversee the cattle operation.

The U-shaped adobe hacienda encloses a courtyard and fountain. This view, looking northeast, shows portions of the original center section (left) and the east wing (right).

In 1878, Thomas Dibblee added another living room, four bedrooms, and a bathroom to accommodate his family (eventually numbering eight children) when they came to the ranch. This east wing was built to conform to the west wing. A middle section creates a patio on the southerly side of the house, and there are two porches facing this patio.

The large working men's dining room, which has been converted to a living room, is paved with flagstones and has a large fireplace at the end away from the kitchen. The room has a skylight on the north-facing roof. On the other side of the east-facing wing is a long porch that accommodates the morning sun and is out of the wind when the westerlies blow (as is often the case in the fall).

The east wing of Casa San Julian was added to the original adobe house around 1878.

The Casa is adjacent to a creek about one hundred feet away. In this space is a large arbor and picnic tables that are used to entertain friends and occasional groups that come to partake of the relaxing atmosphere on the ranch. Yearly barbecues are prepared in a large barbecue pit on the upper end of the picnic area, under a old, large grape arbor that furnishes shade in the summer.

The house has suffered damage from earthquakes, especially during the 1925 Santa Barbara temblor; another severe quake hit us in 1956. The heavy missiles that fly out from Vandenberg Air Force Base often shake the walls with their vibrations. We are glad the space shuttle will not

The large living room in the center section was used as a dining room for the working men of the ranch during the height of cattle and sheep operations.

take off from that base as the pad was likely to have been constructed on the southernmost reaches of the base, right over the hill from the Casa San Julian.

The barbeque area under a huge grape arbor on the east side of the Casa has been
a popular garthering place for family and friends over the years.

Ranch headquarters, looking northeast, with Casa San Julian and outbuildings at center. San Julian Road (Highway 1) is at bottom. Remnants of the original road through the valley can be seen running from right to left across the center of the picture.

The San Julian Road

THE OLD ROAD through San Julian, as I first knew it, was not the original road up the grade from Las Cruces. The older road, laid out by Alfred Poett, wound its way up the valley of Las Nutrias on the north side of the canyon. In contrast, the road I first knew was on the southerly side of the canyon.

That older road was the scene of an accident involving my grandmother, Francisca Dibblee, and her younger son William. Their buggy tipped over, and she had to walk to Las Cruces for help because Bill was quite badly injured. Both roads commenced at Las Cruces in the Gaviota Pass.

Las Cruces, a village near the confluence of today's U.S. Highway 101 and State Highway 1, was known for nearly seventy years as a village that "even had a post office." The post office was later abandoned. There was an inn at Las Cruces, and a saloon, which went out before my time. The village claimed a blacksmith shop (run by Juan Flores), a general store (owned by Jean Loustalot, he being a son of Jake Loustalot, who had the saloon in the latter part of the last century), and two garages about a half-mile apart, one at each end of the settlement.

The garage at the lower end of Las Cruces was run by a fine mechanic named Gene Hess, whose pretty, buxom wife assisted at the country store.

She was a daughter of Henry Tico, one of the best horsemen I ever knew. His mounts were so well-trained that the slightest touch of the rein on their necks would cause them to turn; they would back, spin around on their hind legs, and perform almost like the Lippizaners. Henry was a descendant of the Ticos, grantees to the huge Ojai Ranch that was lost after the big drought of 1862–64.

The inn near the creek crossing was later purchased by a Cockney innkeeper, whose wife bore him two pretty girls. As teenagers, they used to lounge about in the garden in scant attire. This seems to have lured many motorists into the hospitable bar, where barstools were saddles mounted on stands. The nearby trestle bridge over the Gaviota Creek was constructed of steel and had a crossbeam about fifteen feet above the road.

There were six or eight houses alongside the creek on the way up to Walter Neilsen's garage, which was at the upper end of the settlement, just at the foot of the steep Nojoqui grade. The creek was lined with large and beautiful sycamore trees. A schoolhouse on the west side of the canyon stood on Dibblee lands and served the children from Gaviota, the Hollister Ranch, and Las Cruces. Nearby, in the sandstone ridge to the southwest, was a cave that had been the abode of the now-famous Indian, Fernando Librado, whose fertile brain and good memory John P. Harrington tapped in his research on the Chumash tribes for the Smithsonian Institution. (Fernando had once worked for the Dibblees as a sheepherder and had made some acid comments regarding their social status.)

When the state Highway Department decided to widen and improve the road through the pass in the early '50s, they obliterated the settlement, cut out all the trees, and made a divided highway through the village, even demolishing the country store that had been so useful over the years. The state Highway Department did not want any stopping places along the highway that might slow down motorists, especially near a junction with San Julian Road.

About half a mile west of Las Cruces, San Julian Road crossed the creek on the trestle bridge, wound its way along the southerly side of the canyon and entered Rancho San Julian about half a mile onward. A gate was placed there in order to keep our cattle from straying onto the Hollister property below, but the gate was removed in 1910 when the county took over the road and fenced it off.

A short distance later, it ascended the steeper grade through a wooded parcel of land that had been purchased by the Smith brothers of Santa Barbara. They timbered the place and hauled the wood by wagon to Gaviota. It was then loaded into open railroad cars to be hauled to the Smith's Union Feed and Fuel Company at the foot of Anacapa Street in Santa Barbara. Much of the wood was used for cooking as well as in fireplaces.

Our cousins, the Redingtons, who had a house on the corner of Santa Barbara and Pedregosa streets, were among their customers. There were some who did not believe in paying for wood, and the Redingtons were sometimes the victims of thieves. One day, Jack Redington decided to stop the thievery—he drilled a hole in a piece of wood and filled it with black powder, which was then plugged. Not long after, there was a loud explosion about ten blocks away from their house. No more wood was ever lost.

This stretch of the San Julian road leaving Las Cruces was quite steep and composed of clay soil that became slippery when wet and would stay that way for long periods because of a canopy of oak trees. Moreover, the road sloped toward the outer bank for drainage, causing a passing car to slide toward the lower side. For this reason a motorist had to put chains on his tires to navigate safely when it was wet. A driver ascending the grade, on meeting another coming down, would often stop to let the other fellow pass on the inside; if this were not possible, one of them would have to back to where the road was wide enough to pass.

In our Model T Ford (purchased in 1915), the driver had to keep the pedal depressed in low gear to make it up the grade. The dirt roads of those days were such that it was not unusual to drive at a maximum of twenty-five miles an hour on level ground. I remember thinking how great it would be if we could get up to thirty or even forty miles an hour.

Once we gained the summit of Las Cruces grade, we could see the panorama opening ahead of us down the long valley. The road sloped less on the westerly side and continued for about a mile to Los Yridises, where the gradient decreased. The road crossed Yridises Creek on a wooden bridge, then became more winding as it followed the creek bank. It next spanned the Álamo Creek on a short wooden bridge and continued on toward El Atascoso (the sticky place). There the San Julian Road left the main valley and headed over the hills of El Atascoso and passed through a small grove of wind-blown oak trees where, legend recounts, there was a cache of treasure buried by some *bandidos* in their flight from the law. We often wished to seek the fabled treasure as we passed, but there were no magnetic detectors in those days. Later, the county built a large trestle bridge over the deep El Atascoso arroyo near La Gaviotita, and the new road wound along beside El Jaro arroyo.

The reason there were so many turns and twists in the old roads was because it was so difficult to move large quantities of dirt any distance. Much of the earth-moving was done by pick and shovel, or occasionally a grader pulled by horses or mules. But they managed only to move the dirt sideways; they were not very good at moving dirt forward for any distance. The most efficient of the old implements for such a job was the Fresno scraper. This lowliest of all implements was essentially a large, flat-bottomed half bucket that held about three-quarters of a yard of dirt, with a straight leading edge, a long curving handle on the top, and an iron attachment on each side. When the operator scooped dirt, he would raise the long handle, allowing the cutting edge to dig into and scoop up the dirt. When the bucket was full, he would press down on the handle, allowing the bucket to be dragged along to where it would be dumped. On the return trip, front runners kept the bucket out of the dirt. This was a fairly efficient way of moving dirt for short distances; it is likely that much of the transcontinental railroad beds were constructed in this manner.

The coming of the crawler tractor, with its accompanying scrapers, spelled the death knell of the Fresno scraper; and . . .

> While Ceres' plough since ancient times
> has been extolled in song and rhymes,
> the lowly Fresno, long forgot,
> was cast aside to rust and rot.

Caves in sandstone outcroppings at Las Cuevitas were formed by the wind.

The new county road built in 1910 was fenced. Culverts and bridges were installed by the county, but road maintenance was a problem until gravel from Yridises and El Chorro was used to improve it in the 1920s.

In the early thirties, the county straightened and widened the road, paving the new road with asphaltum on the south side of the arroyo, from Las Cuevitas as far as La Golondrina. In this way, traffic was routed away from the ranch house. But this meant that we would have to construct a bridge over the large barranca. A wooden trestle bridge about sixty feet long was built, but the caving banks by the bulkheads were a constant problem. The old bridge gave way once when a truckload of cattle was being driven across, with the result that several of the cows were killed and many injured in the crash. The bridge was rebuilt and repaired so many times that in 1969 we decided to build large bulkheads of concrete at each side of the creek and a pier in the middle to support four railroad flatcars. This bridge should last quite a while, provided the center pier is kept free of debris floating down the creek in heavy floods.

The old road continued west, past the ranch house, down the lane past our cattle corrals and on toward Las Cuevitas (which refers to a large sandstone cave in a rock outcropping about a quarter of a mile above the road). Just before the cave there was a long bridge that spanned a wide gulch. After the county road was abandoned in favor of the new one across the barranca, we planned to take the bridge down and save the timbers, but the job was postponed too many times.

Eventually, Wilson Dibblee ordered the superintendent to take a crew of men down there to start dismantling the bridge. By the time all was ready and the crew approached the bridge, we rounded a turn to see about twenty men busy dismantling the structure. We stopped on the hillside overlooking the bridge to watch as the crew of army engineers carefully took it down and stacked the lumber on the banks. After about two hours, when the job was completed, we approached the lieutenant who led the gang. His embarrassment knew no bounds when he discovered, to our great amusement, that he had torn down the wrong bridge. Wrong for him, but right for us! We never found out where his assigned bridge was, nor did we much care.

About half a mile beyond was another bridge over the creek at Las Ytias. When that wooden bridge became unsafe, the county tore it down and started the construction of a concrete one to take its place. Signs were placed at the Lompoc and Las Cruces ends of the road stating that there was a ''bridge out,'' which was supposed to send motorists around by way of Santa Rosa Road. But there were still many who thought that they could ford the creek without much trouble, and many got stuck in the muddy crossing. An enterprising farmer living nearby took a team of horses down to pull the cars across the creek for fifty cents a car. When a driver refused to pay and got stuck, the fee immediately rose to one dollar, which was grudgingly paid or his car stayed in the creek.

The old road continued on toward Lompoc on the north side of the creek and close to a steep bank above the barranca. There were several mud slides in the area past El Jaro's entrance, and at times, when heavy rains caused the slippery clay to slide down the hill, the road might be closed for several days. The mud could reach a depth of one or two feet, and when it was shoveled away, more would slide down to take its place.

Beyond, the road crossed La Culebra Creek on a low bridge and continued on toward a steep cut above the creek. The bank on the upper side was six or eight feet high. Henry Costa and Joe Pastor were returning one night from a tavern in Lompoc, and as they passed this steep bank they heard a crunch and felt Henry's open Model T Ford swerve. Stopping the car, the bleary-eyed men looked around to see a buck deer trying to extricate himself from where he had landed in the back seat. The two men agreed that the booze they had just drunk was a bit too strong. As they contemplated the situation, the deer escaped from the car and bounded away, apparently none the worse for the accident.

The new road crossed El Jaro Creek just below the confluence of the main creek and avoided the slide area by keeping on the creek's south side, soon reaching the flats of Salsipuedes about three miles beyond.

Fencing

WHEN the Fencing Law became effective in California in 1882[1] as a result (according to Walker Tompkins) of Hollister's efforts, the Dibblees, who had opposed the law (not being as farsighted as Hollister as to its ultimate advantages), started planning to fence their ranch. Albert Dibblee wrote to his brother Thomas in January of that year "of the need to start fencing our ranch with boards." This would have been a herculean task, since the circumference of the ranch was nearly forty miles and would have necessitated the use of nearly a million board-feet of lumber. Fortunately, barbed wire had been recently invented, and Albert wrote to Thomas of its availability.

Competition became intense between the Roebling Company and its largest competitor, Glidden, for the potential sales of barbed wire were practically limitless. It took a considerable amount of hard selling to convince cattlemen that their cattle could be confined by a few flimsy strands of wire. It was usually necessary for a salesman to demonstrate how the wire could contain the cattle. To set up such a demonstration, several acres of land would be enclosed with stout posts and taut wire strung along on the inside of the posts. Then a band of wild cattle would be driven into the enclosure; sometimes a shot would be fired to spook the animals, at which point they would stampede, run into the taut wires, and get knocked down and severely wounded. After a few demonstrations, both cattle and cattlemen would be convinced as to the efficacy of the barbed wire[2]. Although these demonstration fences were generally more secure than those the cattlemen would build on the range, it was an effective way of teaching a large number of skeptical cattlemen that their cattle could be contained by wire.

The early barbed wire was so severe with long, sharp barbs that many animals were badly injured, and it took a regulatory act of Congress to limit the size of the barbs.

Albert Dibblee immediately saw the advantages to the new wire and readily bought it for the ranch. Colonel William Hollister and the Dibblees had separated their interests by that time, and Albert wrote to Thomas that,

> [W]hile Captain Sudden [who had purchased Hollister's La Espada ranch at Honda] would readily pay his share of the fencing, it would be another matter when it came to collecting from Hollister.

Despite the fact that Hollister was a leading exponent of the fencing law, it *was* another matter to collect from the colonel.

By the end of 1883, the Dibblees were completing their purchases of wire, having changed their preference to Glidden wire. Enough was bought to enclose the almost forty-mile boundary of the ranch with six wires—a total of about 240 miles of wire!

Thousands of redwood posts and pickets were purchased for the tremendous job of fencing the ranch. Concern was expressed that Martin Murphy, who owned the adjacent Cojo Ranch at Point Concepción, would balk at paying his share. All the wire was sent down by steamer, most of which landed at the Gaviota Wharf, where it was hauled to San Julian by wagon.

In 1891, the Dibblee brothers separated their interests, with Thomas taking San Julian and Albert taking Jalama. It became necessary to construct more fencing, this time between the San Julian and Jalama ranches. This was not as large a job as fencing the entire San Julian; the boundary between the two ranches was only a little over five miles.

Cattlemen in the plain states were fearful that fencing the open range would threaten their freedom to graze wherever they wished, as had been the case for many years, and they were right.

But another concern for the safety of their cattle was voiced. Cattle on the open range will drift with the storms and can get caught in snow drifts that inevitably form by snow piling up against the fences. Unlike buffalo, cattle had not learned to contend with this problem. Cattle hair, too, is not as protective as that of the buffalo, which contains a woolly down next to the skin. The climate of the buffaloes' American midwest and Rockies is much more severe than that which prevailed in the cattle's native England and Scotland. Snow piling up along fences became a serious problem for cattle in the Midwest, Rocky Mountain, and Plains states.

When the fencing law became effective in Santa Barbara County in 1882, some sheepmen pulled up stakes and left the state. Among those were the Yndarts and Pachecos, who were running sheep on the Alisal in the eastern Santa Ynez Valley.[3] They took their sheep to Nevada and Utah, where they set up a large ranch that came to be known as the YP Ranch. Their first winter there was so severe that they lost many sheep and had to abandon the ranch.

Los Llanitos Ranch, which we used to call Los Encinos, was sold in 1915, to pay off a mortgage the Dibblees had incurred. The lands of Tract A of Rancho San Julian had been set aside for the benefit of Henry Dibblee, but he continued to live at San Julian after the death of his brothers in 1895, and did not seem to want to sell, so at the time of his death in 1910, the tract reverted to the estates of Albert and Thomas.

A man named Leroy Armstrong, on November 3, 1915, first purchased Los Llanitos, which contained a little over two-thirds of Tract A. After a few years Armstrong sold the land to King Gillette (of safety razor fame) and a man named Loundsbury. They, in turn, sold the ranch for $106,000 in the late 1920's to E.M. Nutting, a mining man who ran sheep on the ranch for a number of years. Nutting sold the land around 1933 to the Charles H. Jacksons of Santa Barbara. The Jacksons later purchased the Alisal Ranch from the estate of Charles Perkins, who had held it for some twenty years. The Jacksons bought the YP Ranch in Nevada and shipped cattle here from Nevada with the YP brand on them. Los Llanitos was last sold in 1968 to Louise Moulton Hansen of Orange County.

When the Poetts withdrew from the San Julian operating pool with their land and share of the cattle in 1932, they applied to the Department of Livestock Identification for a brand that designated the name of our ranch (Yridises) combined with Poett. We obtained exclusive use of that brand in our area, and when the Jackson cattle from the YP Ranch in Nevada and Utah were brought down and pastured next to us, they were compelled to rebrand all those cattle on account of the conflicting brands. Jackson sent over his general superintendent, Emmet Edwards (whom I had long known and respected as a friend and a good cattleman), to see if we would sell our brand to them. Emmet chatted with me for about an hour before he broached the subject of the brand, but we were unwilling to sell, as the brand suited us.

Cattle brands used at Rancho San Julian. The three on the top row were registered to José de la Guerra in 1840 (the second was a venta, or counterbrand). The "D" brand was registered in 1866 to the partnership of Albert Dibblee, Thomas Dibblee, and W.W. Hollister. The "SJ" brand was registered in 1919 after the ranch was divided among the Dibblee heirs.

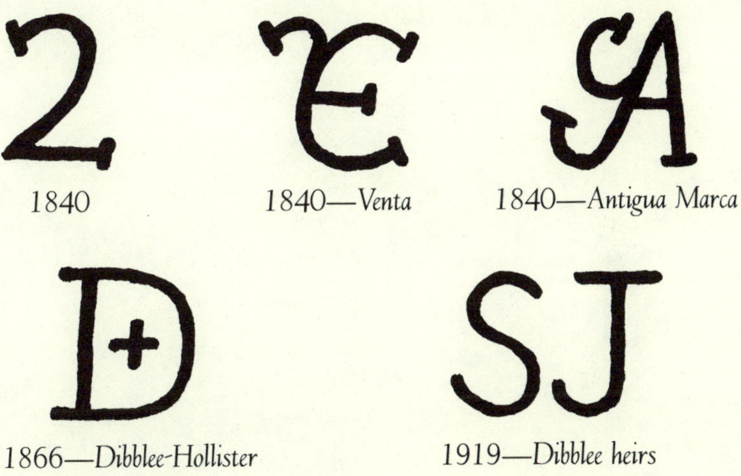

1840

1840—Venta

1840—Antigua Marca

1866—Dibblee-Hollister

1919—Dibblee heirs

Some of the well-galvanized ribbon wire that was purchased in the middle 1880's still remains on our fences, especially the ones farthest from the ocean, where the salt air does not affect it as much as on the westerly or southerly sides of the San Julian. I believe there are redwood posts still in the ground after a hundred years. The posts from the earlier redwoods were more durable than the present ones because more of them came from the heartwood of the trees.

A fence crew consisting of four or five men was maintained at San Julian until the late 1930's. This crew was led by a Basque named Juan Laranetta, who had only one good eye, but with that one eye he could set a straighter fence than most people could with two. The crew went on their excursions in a buckboard and, as it was too difficult and time-consuming to get home for meals, they generally carried several days' rations with them. In the early days, most of the posts were wood and had to be put in holes dug by hand. If my memory serves me correctly, steel posts came into use about the middle 1930's. Wire was about 12.5 gauge. A spool of barbed wire weighed about ninety pounds and used to cost $5 to $7 a spool. Now the cost is nearly $35 a spool.

The Wharf at Gaviota

URING THE Spanish and Mexican occupation of California, there were no wharves or docks along the California coast. Everything had to be brought in or taken out by lighter. This meant that millions of hides had to be carried to the lighter by men who held the hides over their heads to prevent them from becoming wet. Wet hides, of course, soon spoiled when stacked on a ship. Before roads were built to San Julian, the families generally arrived at the ranch from Santa Barbara by way of steamer.

Albert and Thomas Dibblee decided that a wharf at Gaviota would save them a lot of money and time. Since 1872 and the construction of John Stearns wharf in Santa Barbara, their sheep and cattle had been driven and their wool hauled to Santa Barbara to be shipped from Stearns Wharf (in which Hollister held an interest). The Dibblees attempted to obtain Hollister's consent to a wharf at the nearer Gaviota spot. But Hollister was reluctant to pour more money after bad, and for a while he refused. The partners persisted, however, and pointed to the heavy tonnage of wool they were producing. So Hollister finally gave his consent. After obtaining a permit from the board of supervisors, the partners hired Thomas Bard of Hueneme to advise them on the best place and other considerations about a wharf. Construction was started in

Gaviota Landing as it appeared around 1875. Cattle corrals can be seen at left center; a sailing ship lies at anchor offshore.

early 1875 at Gaviota and finished the same year. It was not long before they were handling grain, mutton, wool, and other merchandise from the Santa Ynez Valley, sending it off to San Francisco, whence it would be shipped east by rail.

A group in Lompoc decided that they, too, should have a wharf, and planned to build one at a place called Lompoc Landing, near the mouth of the Santa Ynez River, then called the Purísima. Albert Dibblee warned them that they would not be successful with a wharf there because of the strong northwesterly winds and heavy tides, but they thought he did not want competition with the Gaviota Wharf and disregarded his advice. The Lompoc group built the structure, only to see it swept away by a storm. They persisted and rebuilt, but the coastal passenger steamers would not tie up at the wharf on account of the heavy seas. John B. Ward, who owned El Cojo Ranch near Point Concepción, also threatened to construct a wharf on his ranch, but Albert Dibblee knew that Ward was just bluffing, for Dibblee was aware that the ocean bottom was too deep there and it would be too costly.

For several years the Dibblees and Hollister continued to use the wharf despite heavy costs in maintenance and repair that had to be done after a docking ship hit the wharf and caused extensive damage; the wharf was also damaged by a strong southeasterly storm. They purchased a steam-driven pile driver and obtained pilings from Puget Sound for the repair work. A warehouse had been built on the land end of the wharf to house grain and supplies, and a corral for the livestock that were in increasing demand by the northerners. They hired a wharfmaster named Miguel Burke to run the enterprise for them.

In 1882, a narrow-gauge line from Port Hartford near San Luis Obispo to Los Olivos was built; the farmers of the valley then shipped livestock and produce by rail, to the detriment of Dibblee and Hollister, who could not compete with it.

Damage to the Gaviota Wharf was a recurring worry. When the wharf was under repair, they would take advantage of the railroad at Los Olivos to ship livestock. But, as Joseph Cooper would not let the Dibblees drive their cattle over his Santa Rosa Ranch, the cattle had to be taken by way of Alisal. Once loaded on the railroad cars, and because the trainmen were apt to be rough in handling cattle if a representative of the owner was not around, one of the ranch hands would go along with the cattle. The rail journey to Port Hartford generally got the animals to the ship before sailing time so that they reached San Francisco early the following morning.

A man named McNeilly later became wharfmaster, and a small hotel was constructed to accommodate passengers who embarked or debarked there. Earlier, a stage line from Lompoc had been inaugurated to carry passengers and mail to Gaviota, and the route went through San Julian. This enabled the Dibblees and Hollister to keep in good communication with San Julian, headquarters for their large sheep operation. But it also meant a heavy burden was imposed upon the partners to maintain seventeen miles of road through their ranches. It was not until 1910 that the county took over the road and saw to its maintenance and repair.

The Dibblees, and sometimes Hollister, continued to use the wharf until the railroad came early in 1903. The land at the mouth of Gaviota Canyon was then deeded by the partners' interests for a ten-acre county park. The jointly owned land near Gaviota, extending to the west and above the railroad tracks, continued to be held jointly by the three family groups until the Hollisters sold all of their property interests in the late 1960's.

Thereafter the State of California, desirous of obtaining more land for a state park, brought condemnation proceedings against the owners. An attorney tried to persuade a jury that an atomic reactor would soon be in operation somewhere along the California coast and implied that Point Concepcion would be the logical place for such a reactor. But the jury would not buy that line of reasoning.

However, we were pleased with the award, and the state acquiesced also. Besides our eighty-three-acre interest, the state acquired another large piece of property extending into what we used to call the Santa Anita Slopes (belonging to the Dibblees). The Gaviota property was the last bit of land held jointly by the Dibblee-Hollister interests.

The Gas Pipeline

EARLY IN 1926, Thomas Dibblee's eldest son Wilson (who had become ranch manager) was approached by Robert Easton of Santa Maria Gas Company and officers of Southern Counties Gas Company to explore the possibility of negotiating a right-of-way for a gas line through San Julian. The gasline would serve the large and expanding diatomaceous earth plant near Lompoc. The existing line from Santa Maria could not then supply sufficient gas to meet the needs of this huge enterprise, which used gas kilns to dehydrate the diatomaceous earth. The larger gas fields around Santa Maria had not yet been discovered and surpluses of the fuel were being found near Santa Barbara and farther south.

Bob Easton, an astute businessman whom Wilson Dibblee had known for many years, had been the manager for the Howard-Lansdale families' Chowchilla Ranch in the San Joaquin Valley, where the Dibblees long ago had purchased shorthorn cattle. Ted Howard had great respect and affection for Easton, whose ability as a ranch manager was well known.

The relationship was terminated suddenly one day in 1915 in a tall building in San Francisco when an elevator in which Easton and Howard were riding crashed to the ground. Ted Howard, a tall, strapping man, instantly sized up the situation and grabbed a hold onto Easton, a smaller man, to break his fall and thus saved the latter's life. Easton was severely injured in the crash in which Howard died.

While living there, Easton saw the need for a well-financed gas company and put his many talents to work to accomplish that end.

After agreeing to the conditions for a right-of-way, the gas company hired an engineer to head a survey party, and the Santa Maria Gas Company made an affiliation with Southern Counties Gas Company to assist in financing the large project. This meant building a gas line up the coast from Goleta, where the Ellwood fields had been producing gas for a few years and the huge More well had been blowing for over a year.

The man they hired as chief engineer was Franco Fenzi of Santa Barbara's well-known Fenzi family. Franco, a handsome and well-educated young man, was a great raconteur and always welcome at San Julian, where many a pleasant evening was spent in his charming company. The Franceschi-Fenzi family had come to Santa Barbara from Florence, where Franceschi's brother was a banker. Dr. Franceschi, an eminent botanist, left his mark on Santa Barbara with the introduction of many species of trees and plants.

By the agreement worked out with the landowners, the gas companies were to receive a right-of-way in perpetuity through San Julian. In return they agreed to pipe gas to any occupied residence on the ranch that lay within a mile of the main line and, in addition, to furnish free of charge to the ranch house refrigerators and stoves to supplant the old wood and oil-burning stoves. Gas lights were installed at company expense. It was a great relief to have the lights, as lamps and candles had been used for some years.

My uncle Bill Dibblee was a "night owl," and soon took advantage of the piped gas to construct an electric system. An engine and generator were installed, and electricity was generated with the use of the cheap, clean, efficient gas. Uncle Bill would putter around most of the night in the engine room after the rest of us had gone to bed. Electricity was nearly always available because, besides the engine and generator, there was a set of batteries to furnish light when the engine was not running.

The gas line entered Rancho San Julian just above the upper bridge in the Gaviota Pass. The ditch for this line slowly snaked its way up the steep hillside of the Santa Anita Slopes toward the ridge escarpment overlooking the valley of Las Nutrias, where the eastern terminus of the San Julian Road meets the state highway at Las Cruces.

The Mexican laborers digging the ditch, many of whom were green to that kind of work, complained vociferously about the hard digging. *"Carramba, que tierra tan dura,"* and it *was* hard, but they went doggedly on. Many, if not all of these men were, I believe, *mojados* (illegal aliens) who by their furtive glances toward any stranger practically gave away their illegal status.

The first week was the hardest for those who had not recently wielded pick and shovel, but once their hands were calloused and backs and limbs strengthened by the hard work, they became more relaxed and talkative and sometimes had to be restrained. Many of them would lay down their tools in order to gesticulate while talking, and much labor would thus be lost. They often asked the boss of the diggers to bring them some *cervesa* (beer) from the nearby Las Cruces store and would wink knowingly about his frequent visits there to see the pretty, buxom woman who dispensed the beer.

But he never brought the men the beer they asked for. Instead, they were furnished with cool fresh water from a barrel by a water boy. Once work was over, they flocked to the store for their beer.

The engineers laid the route of the pipeline to avoid landslides and washouts, and this meant going along the ridge tops or near thereto. Through brush, trees, and rocks went the line, closely paralleling the fence that had once been the southerly boundary of the San Julian land grant. The Santa Anita Slopes had been purchased by the Hollister-Dibblee partnership when a government survey determined that portion of land to be government domain, because it lay between the southerly boundary of the San Julian and the northerly boundary of Santa Anita and consisted of about two thousand acres.

To say that the land is steep is an understatement. On the north side of the ridge, the break is almost sheer with a slope of perhaps two to one, or about fifty percent. The south slope is not quite as steep but steep enough so that one day a cylinder of oxygen, which had slipped out of the hands of the man unloading it, went rolling and spinning down the slopes, bouncing on rocks and trees in the wildest gyrations imaginable, until it came to rest about a quarter of a mile away in a deep and rocky ravine covered with almost impenetrable brush—and didn't explode! Everyone watched in amazement, but no one offered to retrieve the cylinder, nor was there an order given for that purpose. I assume that it remains there to this day.

The gas line entered the San Julian in the Gaviota Pass, and left the ranch about nine miles farther at El Jaro. Where the land was not as steep, a ditch digger took the place of the laborers, and this meant about six times as much progress each day. The line was suspended across wide creeks or arroyos and passed within about three quarters of a mile from the ranch house.

My job was to make sure that the pipe was buried over four feet deep and to see that fences and gates were properly repaired when breached. The depth requirement was to assure that the pipe would not be hit by any implement, especially in the farming land.

Several years later, cathode stations were installed to introduce a charge of electricity into the line so as to neutralize the reaction of the iron pipe with acids in the soil. This has worked well, and repairs to the line have been minimal. It still supplies the Johns-Manville diatomaceous earth operations, and the surplus gas is piped to Lompoc and Santa Maria.

Rancho San Julian:
Life on the Ranch

The Men of San Julian

N O HISTORY of Rancho San Julian would be complete without telling of the men who served here so long and faithfully. The hours were long and the work hard at San Julian, but the food was always good. Despite the ongoing wage of $60 a month up until the mid-1930's, most seemed satisfied with the work.

One of the most colorful of these was Alfredo Espinosa, who worked on the ranch for almost forty-five years and in Santa Barbara as the Dibblees' cook for ten more. Alfredo had little if any schooling but taught himself to read and write in both Spanish and English. His habit of gesticulating with his hands and arms was particularly pronounced and helped him express his thoughts. Once, while holding a ladder on which Bill Dibblee was perched near a cactus patch, Alfredo started a discourse on the stars and forgot to hold the ladder steady: Bill tumbled into the prickly patch.

Alfredo's long years as a sheepherder resulted in the not-uncommon habit of talking to himself, as did many of his fellow herders. He would reply to a comment, often carrying on long conversations with himself, not being self-conscious about the apparent eccentricity.

No one, including Alfredo himself, knew his exact age, but early records show him working at San Julian as early as 1887, when he must

Alfredo Espinosa

have been about fifteen years old. He served in such varied capacities as sheepherder, stable man, chore man, gardener, and stand-in cook when there was a crisis in the kitchen or if the cook was away. He served willingly in each of these jobs, albeit not without an argument, ending with the usual chuckle on his part.

The most trivial request or order to Alfredo was invariably followed by a short period of silence in which he composed an argument to oppose the request. It seemed that the basis of his argument was to test the request's validity, although I suspect that it was often just to get one's goat or to find a reason why it could be left for later, or just for the sake of an argument: to pit his wit against yours. At times, it was less trouble to do the job oneself, if the time wasted in arguing would amount to more than it was worth. Threats or intimidation were useless because, having been sent away, his absence was worse than the alternative. In short, Alfredo was virtually indispensable, and he knew it.

From time immemorial, Alfredo, not alone among the men on the ranch, would occasionally imbibe immoderately, so that part of the ensuing day was lost to productive labor. These periods were infrequent and usually occurred on weekends. The worst inconvenience was that someone else would have to milk the cows or tend the chickens for a day or two. There were seldom recriminations, and the lapses were taken as a matter of course.

Alfredo was always around to help as cook and servitor at the frequent barbecues, and he was always ready to help entertain the guests by dancing a jig (which he did with a certain *élan*), telling a story, reciting some poetry he had composed, or making discourse upon some current event—without a bit of self-consciousness. Had he been able to play an instrument or sing, he would have been a great minstrel, for he could improvise with his great wit. His ability to characterize made him more than a clown. He was a jester and loved the role, as did his audience.

Like some other old-timers, Alfredo had a certain instinct about the weather, due to long and careful observation. On occasion, when asked if he thought it would rain, he would reply, "The little frog he sing, the owl she pass by, Pico has rheumatism in the left leg. When he gets it in the right leg, it will rain like hell."

Santiago Rios, or Jim, as he was fondly known to all of us, came to work at San Julian as a *vaquero* in 1883 under Ezequiel Ortega, and succeeded as cattle boss when Ortega left a few years later. He faithfully held his job until blindness forced his retirement after working on San Julian for more than fifty years.

The cattle were gentle and easy to work during Jim's time as head *vaquero*, compared to later years. Jim would always talk to the cattle on approaching them, and they were never spooked by a rider's presence. Jim taught us to ride, but was unprepared for our unorthodox way when we scorned a saddle and discarded the bridle to ride Indian style, a practice he strictly forbade when there were cattle to drive. If our horses became unruly, we would reach down around their necks and pinch off their wind, causing them to stop or slow down.

Much of the riding consisted of checking the cattle. Jim could spot a sick or lame animal a long way off simply by observing its position or stance in the herd. A sick or lame animal will often keep away from other cattle, or hold its head in a droopy position.

Jim would leave the stables each day with a shovel but never have it on his return. Since there were always water troughs to check and maintain, in this way he would have a shovel at nearly every spring, so that the mud there could be dug out to keep the water flowing into the troughs. The first water troughs were nearly all of redwood, and would warp if the water did not flow into them constantly. It was a real headache keeping all of the four or five dozen troughs in order.

Jim nearly always rode his horse at a jog-trot, but when he wanted to roll a cigarette, he would slow the horse to a walk, pull out a sack of Bull-Durham from his breast pocket, and deftly peel off a piece of cigarette paper from the side of the sack. Holding the paper in one hand and the sack of tobacco in the one holding the reins, he would sprinkle tobacco into the curled paper and with one hand roll the cigarette, stick it in his mouth, get a match from his shirt pocket, and strike it swiftly on his *chaparreras* (chaps, as they are now called). After lighting a cigarette, the match would be extinguished and held in his cupped hand before being discarded, to make sure there were no embers.

This calls to mind the story of a man walking over the San Marcos Pass. He was accosted by a *bandido*, who, thinking him a Yankee, held a gun on him despite the latter's protestations that he was a Chileno. The man slowly put his hand in his left hind pocket and, after a moment or two, while being held at gunpoint, slowly withdrew his hand with a cigarette he had rolled in his pocket. At that, the *bandido* roared with laughter and said, "You are indeed a Chileno, for no *gringo* could do that."

Jim was fond of telling tales of the old days—how the grizzly bears were challenged by the long-horned bulls, how Dan Guevarra chased a mountain lion up a sycamore tree with only a hammer to throw at the beast, how Vincente Guevarra rode his bucking horse down that steepest of all hills on El Jaro. "By jorry," Jim would say, "in them days a man really had to ride his horse."

Sitting beside the fire on long winter evenings, we listened, enthralled, as Jim, Alfredo Espinosa, and Marcello Pico reminisced and told their stories of days long past, the "good old days"—referring to the days before the automobile, which seemed a menace to many old-timers, for they sensed an irreversible change due to the auto and were not so sure that it was for the best.

Jim Rios loved the land, the cattle, and the ranch, and he left us with a precious legacy, as did our mother, aunts, and uncles. A friend accuses me of being sentimental about the land (to which I gladly plead guilty), and I see that many of my nieces, nephews, and cousins, some after having gone to the big cities, now have the same attachment to the ranch.

Marcello Pico was about Jim's age and had been on the ranch longer than almost anyone can remember. He was the head teamster, whose function was to supervise and train the younger men who came to "team" on the ranch. He did not have to break the horses (a long and tedious job done by the professional horsebreaker, Charlie Williams), but Pico generally took charge of the newly broken teams and seldom had any runaways.

The Clydesdale horses were usually gentle and easy to work. We had many mares, which were bred to Barney, the huge stallion of the same breed. He had his own enclosure, which was nearly like a stockade, with a high fence down at the end of the horse barn. Once in a while, Barney would be bred to a good-size saddle mare, resulting in a rather large cross-bred saddlehorse. Most of our saddlehorses, however, were American saddlebred or thoroughbred; we generally bought the former from the Hollisters.

Pico drove the large freight wagons to Lompoc to take the beans to the warehouse or bring back lumber or other cargo, and as children we were sometimes allowed to go with him. Sitting on the high seat beside Pico, with our short legs dangling, my sisters, Frederica and Nan, and I savored the long and adventurous drive over the often bumpy and nearly always dusty road to Lompoc. The teams walked nearly the whole way to town and back, a distance of about twenty-four miles that took all day.

The beans were delivered to the S.P. Milling Company warehouse next to the railroad; generally a load of lumber and some wire or posts would be hauled back to the ranch. The S.P. Milling Company had a virtual monopoly on these items and the owners were apt to be ornery in their dealings, until the upstart Lloyd Moore bought a small lumber yard in 1946 from a man named Stephenson, who had been unable to run the yard because the war made it difficult to get lumber. Lloyd Moore eventually ran the other firm out of the lumber business by accommodating the needs of the people of Lompoc and surroundings. Although they continued as warehousers for many years, few mourned the demise of S.P. Milling as lumbermen.

After discharging the cargo and loading freight for the return trip, Pico would drive through the main streets of Lompoc, where he would stop for mail and always buy us a package of delicious Nabisco cookies, which we ate on the way home. We often became drowsy on the return trip and would get down from the high seat to lie on the burlap sacks that were bought to hold beans. Generally our sleep was interrupted by a bump in the road or a passing automobile, either of which could cause a cloud of dust. If the wind blew, which was usually the case, we approached a certain overhanging oak tree with some trepidation: a tin sign nailed high on the tree would often moan ghostlike in the wind and scare the horses.

The road was narrow and winding, and Pico had to take care lest he allow the wagon to get too close to the steep bank above the creek. With the approach of an automobile at some narrow place in the road, the driver of the auto was supposed to take the outside, in order to eliminate the chances of the horses shying and causing the wagon to slide over the bank. Some automobile drivers did not realize the hazard involved, and were often impatient when the teamster stood his ground.

As Marcello Pico reached old age, the arthritis in his back became so bad the poor fellow could not stand erect, and he had to leave the ranch. Two of his sons, Abel and Alejandro, who worked on the ranch previously and were drafted in World War I, came back and continued working at San Julian until the late 1920's, as did Delfino Gonzalez.

There were so many workhorses on the ranch that a harness maker was employed full time to make and repair harnesses. Occasionally, he would have time to construct or repair a saddle, but I never remember him carving out a saddle tree, which would be done from a piece of sycamore or willow wood. We generally purchased a Visalia tree saddle, which seemed to be the best for those days.

Charlie Williams's method of breaking a workhorse consisted of first bridling the animal and driving it around in circles for hours at a time, so that the beast would readily respond to the pull on the reins from the man on the ground. Then, if the animal seemed to respond well enough to this procedure, he would put a harness on it and hitch the horse to another gentle horse. He would repeat the process, driving the animal in circles, with the gentle one on the inside, all the while repeating ad infinitum, "Whoa, Nellie, whoa, Nellie," in a soothing voice. I can almost hear his voice to this day repeating the message to Nellie, Rosie, or Chubby, as he pulled on the reins of the bridle, which was always a straight bit or a snaffle bit without the curb used on riding horses.

When the horse was deemed sufficiently gentle for the cart, he would hitch it to the long shalves of the breaking cart. They were long so that, if the animal kicked, it would not be able to hit the vehicle, which was sturdily built and low slung, and therefore difficult to overturn. The cart did not have very good springs, for that might have made it less stable.

Generally the horse would start off at a brisk trot, sometimes with a rider beside to help guide or restrain the novice, and after a trot of a mile or two, the animal generally quieted down, hot and sweaty from nervousness.

A good teamster would never lay down the reins of his team unless he was pretty certain that the horses would not run away, for a vehicle, plow, or farm implement could be wrecked and a horse badly hurt.

The cattle king Henry Miller, who was out riding one day on one of his large ranches, came to a gate near where a young man was tilling a large field with a six- or eight-horse team. Miller called for the fellow to come over and open the gate so that he would not have to dismount, but the young man refused on the grounds that his team had some young horses and might run away. Miller let himself through the gate and on his

Our Holt Caterpillar tractor at work. The rider on horseback is Alex Able, foreman, and the man standing on the equipment is John Flickinger.

arrival at headquarters asked after the young fellow. "He is a good man. Give him a raise," said Miller.

The coming of large-scale farming, caused by the heavy demand for beans during World War I, brought about a change to more efficient methods of farming, which demanded the use of the tractor. Around 1916, Wilson Dibblee invested in a Holt Caterpillar. This huge machine took the place of six six-horse teams, although workhorses were still used to cultivate and cut the beans, pull the bean wagons, mow and rake hay, and do other functions not adaptable to the big tractor. (Rubber-tired tractors were still several years in the future; it was not until the 1930's that their use became widespread.)

Until the pickup harvester became available in the late 1940's or early fifties, we used a large stationary harvester at San Julian that was pulled and operated by the Holt caterpillar. John Flickinger, a good mechanic and driver (trained by the Caterpillar Company to run their machinery), came to work for us and stayed about ten years. He kept the harvester in

Bean harvesting on the ranch, ca. 1915.

such good condition that I do not ever remember a breakdown during harvest or plowing time.

As many as twenty men were needed to thresh the beans. Besides the mechanic, there were six teamsters to drive the wagons, four to six men to pitch the beans into the wagons, two men on the table where the beans were dumped, a man with a team to pull the net up from the wagon to dump the beans, a sack sewer, a man to buck the sacks, another to spread the chaff with a team of horses, and perhaps one or two more. My sister Ynez ("Nan") and I were delighted to help drive the wagons; we were only fourteen and fifteen years old at the time, but experienced with horses. Of course, our teams were the gentlest of the lot.

Often, bean threshing lasted late into the night. There was always the chance that early rains would come and spoil the crop; once rained on, the beans were difficult to thresh or would become moldy or discolored and bring a lower price.

C.E. Russell came to work in 1922, but shortly thereafter returned to his home in Canada after the death of his father. He came back again in

C.E. Russell

1926, about the same time as the Irishman Henry "Mac" McLean. Russell worked as a teamster, but was soon promoted to truck driver when a new Kleiber truck with solid tires was purchased in the late 1920's. This truck was a sturdy and heavy vehicle that supplanted the freight wagons and transported beans to Lompoc and returned with the freight. The trip by truck was made in about three hours instead of eight or ten by wagon. Our truck was not large enough to haul cattle, and so did not have cattle racks. We continued to drive our cattle to Gaviota and, later, to Drake.

C.E. Russell could do anything on the ranch, include ride, and soon he became indispensable. In the early 1950's, he was made superintendent of the ranch, a position he held until retiring in about 1983. He died in August 1990.

A retiring and modest fellow, Russell was well-liked by everyone, and not one to throw his weight around. He would do any job that needed to be done, and was always on hand in case of emergency. He married my sister Nan in the middle thirties and lived in a cottage near the schoolhouse, where they raised three children.

There were many other men who worked on San Julian, of course. I hope some day to compile a list of these men who gave so much of themselves and made San Julian a viable entity, so that they may be honored over the years, and their names not be forgotten.

SHEEPHERDING

THERE may be occupations lonelier than sheepherding, but they would be difficult to name.

On the Dibblee and Hollister ranches there were between sixteen and twenty sheep camps spread over the forty-eight thousand acres, each camp comprising a flock of between two thousand and three thousand sheep. In the early days, the herders were Spaniards, Mexicans, Americans, and a few Chinese and Indians. Their names read like those of the *conquistadors*: Cléofas Ponce de León, Manuel Hernández, Isidro Montaña, and Ezequiel Ortega. There were such oriental names as Cheh Tung and Ah Lung, and a few Indians without surnames, such as Estéban, Andrés, and José. Andrés was buried in a small plot on a hill overlooking the Casa de San Julian.

At each sheep camp, there was a one-room board-and-batten shack about twelve feet by fifteen feet with a wood-burning stove, a table, a chair, a cupboard, and a bed. There was no piped water, but each camp was located near a flowing stream or fenced spring from which the occupant carried water in a pail. There was always an outhouse about forty feet from the shack.

Not far from the shack was the sheep corral, which usually consisted of a large wind-row of brush and tree trimmings laid in a circular pattern, with a high panel gate at the gap nearest the cabin. This type of enclosure offered better protection for the sheep than a wire corral through or over which predators might slip unnoticed. The brush pile was usually too broad for an animal to leap over and too dense for a coyote or lion to slip through. Bears were sometimes a problem, but their numbers had been greatly reduced by the mid-1870's.

The shepherd's dog slept in a protected spot, usually under the shack, from where it could slip out at the approach of a predator. These faithful dogs were ever on the alert, and any stirring of the flock during the night usually brought out the dog, sniffing the air for signs of an intruder or growling to warn one away.

In the daytime, the dog usually kept close to his master, watching the flock for strays, and when any animals strayed too far off, the dog, often without command, would trot off to return the wayward sheep to the fold, sometimes with a nip on the flank as a warning.

These dogs were mostly collies or the black-and-white curly haired shepherds from the English-Scottish border. A man would never part with a good sheep dog. The Basques from Spain always seemed to prefer

Sheep on the San Julian hills

dogs that had a dew-claw. It is doubtful that sheep raising, as practiced on the Western ranges, would have been successful without these faithful and intelligent dogs.

At camp, the shepherd rose at dawn and, after breakfast, rain or shine, would open the corral gate to release the sheep. The lambs, if there were any in the flock, scampered out first and gamboled awhile as their anxious mothers bleated for them in vain. Finally, their exuberance gratified, they would return to their mothers to nudge them in the udder for a suckle of milk. The dogs did not pay much attention to the playful lambs, knowing they would soon return to the fold.

As the area near the camp was generally fed short, the sheep would head away to better feeding grounds, starting off at a trot, until they reached a place where the grass was taller. There they would graze, gradually moving in a band toward the shade or a stream if the weather was hot or warm. Around noon the flock would generally lie or stand in the shade, chewing their cuds, or seek water until hunger again overcame them or the day cooled off enough for them to be in the sun.

During this period of heat and rest, while the sheep were not apt to stray, the herder would drowse while the sheep ruminated or he would sometimes return to camp for lunch. Alfredo Espinos was the one herder who would carry a book or magazine with him to occupy himself while at rest. His reading was slow and tedious as he quietly read each word.

Twice a month, a rider from headquarters came with his packhorse to provide the camp with potatoes, onions, coffee or tea, sugar, flour, and perhaps some fresh fruit or vegetables. Also brought was a good portion of jerky, corned beef, or pickled beef tongue. The herder was allowed to slaughter for his need a sheep or lamb, which he would consume before the next visit of the rider.

As shearing time approached, word of when to expect the men who made the rounds would be relayed by the Caire family on Santa Cruz Island, where the operations nearly always preceded San Julian.

If the weather remained dry, the whole lot of sheep, numbering between 20,000 and 43,000, would be shorn within fifteen to twenty days. The more distant bands from the Santa Anita, Las Cruces, and

Jalama ranches were brought in and pastured in the nearby fields, then transferred to the main corrals as their turns to be sheared came.

Shearing time at San Julian more than doubled the number of men who needed to be fed, and, as there were usually thirty or more shearers, generally taxed the sleeping and eating facilities.

First to arrive was Florentino Garcia in his buckboard with his dog, bedding, and equipment, and usually a half-dozen of his *compañeros.* Florentino, a fat, jolly fellow with a walrus mustache, always called me "Topsy." Despite his corpulence, he held his own against all shearers. When I first knew him, in 1915, he had been coming to San Julian as a shearer for thirty years. The rest of the shearers straggled in by stage-coach, on horseback, and occasionally on foot, but nearly always ready for the day set to commence shearing.

Shearing such large numbers of sheep required a central location with adequate facilities. This was done at San Julian headquarters, where a large wool barn, three large holding corrals, various pens, a shearing plat-form, and a dip were located in close proximity.

On the appointed day, if most of the shearers had arrived, a nearby band of as many as fifteen hundred head of sheep would be driven to the corrals. About one hundred and fifty of these would be put onto a crowding platform; this was divided into three pens by means of portable panels. The panel gates were then closed to prevent too much milling by the sheep. The shearing floor was adjacent to the crowding pens, but under the roof of the wool barn, a space about fifteen feet wide and one hundred and fifty feet long that allowed room for thirty or so shearers.

When ready, each man would enter the crowding pen, grab a sheep by its hind leg, and pull it through the small swinging door near him on the shearing floor. There the shearer deftly flipped the animal on its back or haunches and held it in the desired position between the shearer's legs.

Using hand shears—long scissors-like instruments with tapered blades widening to about one and a half inches with a spring action that opened them automatically after closing—the shearer would begin shearing the animal from the underside of the neck and down along the ridge of the

A brass token, later exchanged for pay,
was received by the shearer for each sheep shorn.

breastbone, around the shoulder, and thence along the side of the belly and down the flank. With each clip of his shears, the shearer would cut away two to six inches of wool. The cut wool, still clinging to the uncut portion, would be flipped over with a flick of the wrist to allow the shearer to see his way. If he was careful and did not cut the skin, the animal usually remained calm and the process would be finished in ten to twenty minutes. The wool from the neck, sides, back, and flanks usually came off in one piece, but the shorter wool from the face, legs, and belly scattered and was picked up separately and kept apart so it would not be mixed with the better wool.

After shearing, the animal was released back into the crowding pen with the others. The shearer gathered the main pile of wool and deposited it on a nearby table, receiving a brass token that he later exchanged for his pay. (The rate for shearing in the mid-1880's amounted to fifteen cents a sheep, and a good shearer could make up to $6 or even $7.50 a day.)

The bundle of wool on the table was placed with others in a hopper, whence it was dropped into a baler. The baler was mounted on a platform scale so that the weight of each bale would amount to four hundred and twenty pounds. The baler was run by a screw turned by a long handle, and the bale, when pressed, was tied with steel bands. The wool barn was large enough to hold perhaps one hundred and fifty tons of baled wool.

After all the sheep in the crowding pen were sheared, they were released into a nearby pen that was next to the dip; another lot was brought onto the crowding floor. The pen leading to the dip had a V-shaped chute with solid, high sides. The dip was a submerged vat with redwood sides and bottom and a chute on each end. It was about thirty feet long, eight feet deep, and four feet wide, with the sides projecting two feet above the ground. A sloping ramp lined with smooth iron covered the ground at the approaching side so that the animals, which were crowded into this portion of the chute, slid head-first into the dip. Upon surfacing, the sheep would swim quickly to the other end, which had a gently sloping, cleated ramp leading off to another corral.

About thirty feet from the dip, on the lower side, was a large wood-fired boiler with underground pipes connected to and from the dip to warm and circulate the concoction of water, carbolic acid, lime, sulfur, and juice from the stems of the tobacco plant—all of which proved effective in controlling the scab mites and ticks that infested sheep and cattle.

The sheep were always dipped after shearing and at any time when scabies became prevalent. In the latter case, they would have to be dipped three times at intervals of two or three weeks to control the infestation, which could spread to other sheep.

After dipping, the sheep were placed in the corral that held their lambs. In a few minutes the bedlam of bleating lambs would be diminished as lamb and ewe mothered up.

While the lambs were separated from their mothers at shearing time, their tails would be docked (cut off) and the males altered (the resulting wound was treated with the carbolic acid concoction). Care had to be taken to keep the wound clean on account of the prevalence of tetanus, which is ever-present in dirt in which the feces of sheep or cattle are dropped.

When the foxtail and rip-gut grasses spread over the ranges and predominated in years of slight rainfall, or the clover did not germinate well due to the lack of heavy rains, these grasses did great damage to the sheep. The seed pods of the foxtail and rip-gut brome, being sharp and

Alfredo Espinosa and flock of "my sheep" in front of Rancho San Julian School.

barbed, would be propelled into the flesh by movement of the wool, often causing wounds that became infested with the screw worm.

In the days before the Spaniards, California and much of the southwest was populated with grasses that were mostly of the bunch-grass type of perennials. These were lightly grazed on by deer, squirrel, rabbits, and tule elk, all of whose populations were kept in balance by the Indians and predators of the region. These grasses were easily uprooted or overgrazed when cattle and sheep were eventually intro-duced. The burr clover and alfileria, which had come over from the Mediterranean with the sheep to Mexico, wrought great change on the ecology by quickly spreading on the ranges and allowing heavier grazing. The seeds of the burr clover, being oil-bearing, do not germinate with only light rain and sometimes remain dormant for decades until saturated by heavy rains. Even then, some of the seeds remain for years. I have seen fields, which had been kept clean-cultivated for twenty years, become covered with profuse stands of burr clover when abandoned.

The early bunch grasses consisted of hardy perennial types, a few annuals, and short-lived perennials. Of the hardier species, some of which exist today in scattered locations on the ranges, is the *Elymus* (western rye), the seeds of which the Indians used for food. There are several varieties of this grass, ranging from the coarse giant wild rye (*E. condensatus*), which has an arsenic stage and is seldom grazed, to the more succulent blue wild rye (*E. glaucus*), found along the West Coast from British Columbia through California and into Nevada and Montana. This latter rye can stand heavy grazing because it is deep-rooted, grows in heavy soil, and spreads mainly by underground roots, although one finds occasional seed pods. The blue wild rye likes moist heavy soil. The less-hardy bunch grasses were the *Stipas*, of which there are still about twenty varieties in scattered locations in California. Remaining green much of the year, these grasses were eagerly sought out by the sheep in the dry season and thus over-grazed or uprooted.

The burr clover and *Alfileria* (filaree) can withstand heavy and sustained grazing. Burr clover seeds, being hard, often pass through sheep or cattle and are spread over the ranges. The spreading of these grasses thus permitted a large increase of sheep and cattle on the ranges.

Another flock in front of Rancho San Julian School, about 1912. Clarence Randall, teacher, stands third from left in back row. To his left, Augustin Rios. In front row, second from right, is Mercedes "Nanice" Poett and to her right, A. Dibblee Poett.

As time passed, the price of wool fell due to competition from Australia and New Zealand, the damaging foxtail and rip-gut brome became prevalent on the ranges, and the area became less hospitable to sheep. The cattle industry was making a comeback from the disasters that had all but wiped it out in the early 1860's.

Many cattlemen on the western ranges viewed the encroachment of sheep as a menace to the dominance of the grasslands and started a myth that sheep and cattle would not graze on the same land. This patently spurious rumor gained wide credence and prevailed for many years, but was scoffed at by us as we grazed cattle and sheep on the same ranges for years. Recent studies by agricultural colleges, moreover, tend to disprove this canard by showing that sheep and cattle grazing together offer protection to the sheep from coyotes, if the animals have been brought up together in mixed company.

Cattle Ranching

THE MOST exciting times for us as children on the San Julian were the annual spring rodeos and cattle drives to the railroad that, in the early days, took us through Gaviota Pass. When traffic later increased so that the drives became too hazardous, we would take our cattle over the hills at La Gaviotita and down the steep incline of the Hollister Ranch to the railroad station at Drake. The Hollisters, who had more political clout than we, continued to drive cattle through the pass for another ten years.

The trail down the slopes and through the Hollister Ranch was steep and rocky. There was always plenty of brush from which ticks would vacate onto anything with blood. We seldom, if ever, got bitten by infected ticks from the open areas, as this more often occurs when ticks living in damp areas are affected by Lyme's disease.

We were always on good terms with the Hollisters, although there were a few occasions when we became provoked by them, as they must have occasionally been by us.

One such occasion occurred when the Hollister *vaqueros* brought back a shorthorn bull of ours that insisted on breaking through the boundary fence to visit Hollister's fair white-faced heifers down by the sea. We were not so much annoyed that they brought the bull back as by the

Cattle drive at El Jaro around 1935.

manner in which they did so—it caused the bull's death. The day was hot, and the recalcitrant bull became overheated and refused to move, whereby he was roped tightly—too tightly—by the neck and forced to move to our pasture. There he expired, to the great chagrin of our neighbors, who never heard the end of the tale.

In preparation for the cattle drive to the railroad, marketable cattle would be brought in to nearby pastures from different parts of the ranch over a period of a week or so, and held there in preparation for shipping and weighing. If a deal with a cattle buyer had been made by Wilson Dibblee, an excellent judge of cattle, the cattle were generally held overnight in the scales corral without feed or water. No shrinkage would be taken or, if they had access to feed and water, a shrinkage of about 2 percent would be allowed the buyer. These cattle buyers were excellent judges, and not only as to the condition of the cattle. They could generally out-guess a rancher as to the weights of the animals. Usually they drove around in Cadillacs or Lincolns, attesting to the success of their judgments.

Once, after we sold a shipment of cattle from San Julian and were preparing to sell more, a buyer came up to me and asked if the cows at the auction yards were the same as the previous week. I replied in the affirmative, to which he said that he could pay up to a cent and a half more for the cows because they had not been allowed to drink out of ponds on the ranch (where lived the spirochete of *leptospirosis* that attacks the liver of cattle, rendering them worth less money).

The original cattle scales were Fairbanks and had been purchased by Wilson's father Thomas Dibblee and Thomas's brother Albert in the middle 1880's. The scales could weigh up to ten tons, although the number of cattle placed on the scale could not reach that figure. They lasted about forty-five years before being replaced. In the days before trucks became prevalent, the scales tester usually came around in his automobile with about five hundred pounds of lead weights, which he

Roundup in Los Amoles Valley around 1940.

would cart onto the scales. He would place the weights at each corner and read the beam before moving on to the next corner. These days, a large truck with a hydraulic or electrical crane backs up to the scale and hoists four five-hundred-pound blocks of lead onto the scales, one corner at a time. The tester checks the beam at each movement of the blocks. This gives an accurate test of the scale; it is done yearly on scales that are used regularly.

Testing will not, however, eliminate over-weighting—such as occurred with one rancher whose dog regularly stayed on the scale with each lot of cattle and thereby earned valuable bonuses for his master. This happened so often without notice that, when one buyer eventually detected the ruse, he blackmailed the rancher, promising not to reveal the affair. The narrator of this story is not now alive to corroborate it, but I do not doubt its authenticity.

On the day of the cattle drive, we arose early, usually by five o'clock, fed and watered our horses, and, after breakfast at six, rode out and gathered the cattle from the holding field, or, if they had been weighed the day before, took them from the corral and drove them on the road to Las Cruces. Usually Wilson Dibblee, five or six *vaqueros*, and two or three of us children made up the contingent of riders.

Up the road toward the east we went, past the Casa de San Julian, the schoolhouse, and on toward La Golondrina. The cattle would usually string out into a half-mile line as the younger and more sprightly animals walked faster than the rest of the drove. The riders were interspersed so that about three or four groups of cattle were pushed along by a couple of riders. As the drives nearly always occurred in the late spring or early summer when the cattle were fat and the roads were dry, the road was nearly always dusty.

In the early days, we kept steers until they were three years old, by which time they might weigh 1,200 pounds. They were then fattened on grass; the practice of fattening cattle in large feedlots, away from the central markets, had not come into general use. Today, most cattlemen in this region sell their steer calves at weaning time; these go directly to the feed lots as weaners at the age of six or eight months. One reason for the

Roundup in the Ytias around 1950

earlier weaning and heavier weights at weaning time is the absence of the screw worm, which used to prevail in the southwest and would attack the calves at birth by getting into the navel immediately after hatching. Their presence, if not soon detected, could cause the calf's death within a short time. This pest was difficult to treat until a gas was found that could be injected directly into the infected place and kill the worms. The U.S. Department of Agriculture found that by trapping and irradiating a large number of male flies, rendering them sterile, the pest's population could be controlled. Most areas where cattle graze in this country are now free of the pest.

The occasional motorist we encountered along the San Julian Road would usually pull off to the side for the ten minutes it took for the cattle to pass. More troublesome were those motorists going the same way as we, for the cattle would often trot along ahead of the autos unless restrained or side-tracked by a rider to allow the car to pass.

At La Golondrina we left the county road and made our way along the pasture side of the fence enclosing the bean fields. Soon the incline became steeper and the day hotter. Though the cattle always sought the shade of the nearby off-road willows, they had to be kept away from those cooler spots. Halfway up the hill was a water trough fed by a nearby spring, which was enclosed with a wire fence. Within the enclosure was a large blackberry bush from which we would partake of

A. Dibblee Poett handling a reluctant steer.

the delicious berries while the cattle tarried at the trough. As a large bovine can drink five or more gallons of water weighing forty or more pounds, it, of course, became harder to urge the cattle on. But we pushed them on to the summit from where, on a clear day, we could overlook the ocean and see as far as the Rincon in Carpinteria. After resting for a few minutes at the top, where there was nearly always a breeze, the cattle would start down the steep eastern slope, where the county road wound its way down the southerly side of the canyon. There the cattle would go pell-mell down the steep slope—driven cattle seldom walk down a steep hill, which they would if left to themselves. After a short rest at another water trough near the road, it was down the county road to Las Cruces; the road was fenced on both sides, so we had no trouble on the descent—unless a motorist was in a hurry to pass.

After reaching the bottom of the grade at Las Cruces, we came to the corrals that we maintained not far from the schoolhouse, and there we stopped to let the cattle rest while we ate our lunch. Beside the road, about a hundred yards from the school, was a blacksmith shop belonging

Cattle branding at Los Amoles around 1940.

to Juan Flores, complete with a forge anvil and all the tools of his trade. Juan was a slightly built and amiable fellow as well as a superb artisan who could fashion a bridle bit inlaid with silver or copper (now collectors' items), or make a set of andirons second to none. He would often drop what he was doing to tighten or replace a loose or lost horseshoe, and then sit down and light a Bull Durham cigarette to chat awhile. He knew the comings and goings of nearly every passerby; messages were sometimes left for him to transmit. When some tramp going by appeared slightly taciturn or uncommunicative, the handy bottle of brandy would usually elicit any information that Juan desired from him. The booze was supplied by his wife, Christina, whose house nearby was a well-known source of the illicit beverage.

Directly across Las Nutrias Creek from Juan's shop stood the defunct saloon of Jake Loustallot that went out with prohibition. Christina took over the surreptitious vending of bootleg booze—we never knew her source.

Joe Pastor was another bootlegger. He farmed at San Julian. He was a happy-go-lucky Portuguese who often went fishing with a friend off Gaviota, where he had some lobster pots. Invariably, when he pulled up the traps, there would be a few bottles of booze in a sack alongside. Seldom, if ever, was he apprehended for bootlegging. Who would guess that under the snapping lobsters in the sack lay the contraband liquor? I think the lobsters he peddled were of higher quality than his liquor.

Resuming the cattle drive, we crossed the trestle bridge over the Gaviota Creek near Las Cruces Inn and then onto the main highway, which before 1918 was a dirt road with little traffic. As it was mostly downhill for about two miles, the cattle made good time along the road, until we came opposite the trestle over Gaviota canyon, where a fairly steep grade slowed us down a bit. Here we encountered perhaps two or three dozen cars and an occasional Greyhound bus. On one occasion, when the driver of a bus did not heed our riders' warning to stop for oncoming cattle, the bus was challenged by a huge shorthorn bull that gouged the bus's radiator and caused a lady passenger to fall off her seat. The bull died and the Greyhound Company was sued by us and the passenger, both of whom collected damages.

Soon we reached the road that took us down to the Gaviota station. Before we reached the railroad tracks, there was a gate that led to the corrals above the embankment next to the tracks. (This embankment made it easier to load the cattle as they did not have to climb a ramp.)

If we were lucky and had the cooperation of the station agent, the railroad cars would be spotted on the siding. We could then load the cattle without having to move any cars. Each cattle car held about forty full-grown cattle, and we always advised the station agent how many cars would be needed to accommodate our cattle. One had to be on good terms with the station agent, for at its best the Southern Pacific railroad did not bother to accommodate the small shipper. (Indeed, the railroad was known throughout the state as the "octopus," which controlled California politics until Governor Hiram Johnson broke the power of the insidious railroad cabal.) We made it a point to take the agent some fruit or fresh vegetables in order to assure that our cars would be there in time—and they usually were.

After loading a car we would have to move it by hand and bring the next car to where the cattle could be loaded. This necessitated the use of a couple of railroad bars or a chain hooked onto our Dodge to get the cars moving. The siding was nearly level, and once someone released the brake wheel the car would start to roll until the open car door came to the cattle chute. Then the brake would be applied and the cattle loaded into the car. If we had more cattle to load, we had to move the two loaded freight cars by repeating the process; the cars would then have to be inched back with the railroad bars, a long and tedious job.

The majority of the riders and all of the horses having been sent home, the rest of us would then go into the spacious and fairly comfortable station waiting room, which had a good iron stove to warm the room with a few scoops of coal. We would settle down to wait for the local freight train to come and pick up the cars. The other freight trains would never stop for a few cars of cattle, and we nearly always had to send someone along to see that the cattle cars would not be shunted off onto a siding and left there for several days, causing the cattle to lose weight or starve to death. With our man on the train, this never happened.

As we waited at the station, we could hear the winds howling down over the mountains, as happens in the spring, summer, and autumn when the land in the interior cools faster than the coastal air, and the warm air is forced to seek a warmer region. These "Sundowner" winds sweeping over the ocean stir up the waters of the channel and bring up nutrients to feed the marine life all along the California coastline from Monterey to Ventura. The most daring of the Yankee skippers often took advantage of these winds to propel their ships up the coast. This was a tricky thing to do, as one had to know exactly where the reefs and rocks lay along the shore, because the winds, being only thermal winds and not belonging to any large wind pattern, did not reach out to sea very far. But they are quite consistent and generally come every evening when the weather is warm inland.

Sometimes the local freight train came early, sometimes late, but whatever time it came, we were there to see that our cattle got off safely. On the rare occasions when the local freight did not pick up our cattle, the station master was obliged to stop the next freight train and have it back onto the siding to take our cars. The train men did not seem to mind. It was only the railroad management that was so ornery.

In those days there was no radio communication between trains or the station master and train crew, other than the station master's ability to activate a few semaphores warning the train to stop. Messages between the station master and a train crew were exchanged by leaving notes on a large hoop, which the passing engineer would scoop off the agent's arm; any communication for the agent would be thrown down near his feet. The station agents were obliged to know Morse code, and all of the messages back and forth were transmitted by code on telegraph lines. This practice continued well into the mid-1940's, and maybe even later.

By the mid-thirties, most of our cattle were hauled to market by truck. While we missed the long drives to the railroad, we would not want that phase of the business to return. Too many pounds of meat were wasted and too much time and energy expended to get our cattle to market.

Cattle Diseases

With the possible exception of the hoof-and-mouth disease, endemic in large parts of Europe, no disease in cattle has struck such terror in the hearts of cattlemen in the West and Southwest as Texas fever (*babesiosis*), also known as bovine malaria (*piroplasmosis*); it is carried and spread by the tick *Boophilus*.[1] It is generally confined to America's tropical regions, but a strain seems to have survived the drier parts of the Southwest and was introduced to California probably in the mid-1880's.

The germ attacks the liver, spleen, lungs, and gallbladder, possibly all at the same time. The infected animal can die within seven to ten days after infection. Calves born to cows living in endemic areas are generally immune to the disease through the transmission of colostrol antibodies. A fairly effective and recent treatment is Trypan Blue, administered in the early stages of the disease.

The effect of the malady on infected cattle was dramatic and heartbreaking to witness. One account tells of a case at the Baron corrals near Tajiguas, where the narrator was looking over a bunch of cattle corraled there. The animals started to die for no apparent reason. Closer inspection would have revealed evidence of acute anemia in the nose and eyes of the animals, or blood in the urine.

So concerned were the Dibblees about the spread of Texas fever onto San Julian that they submitted a bill to the state legislature that was passed, essentially in the form submitted.[2] The bill provided for the creation of an office of state veterinarian to oversee and control the movement of infected cattle and mandate the dipping of cattle in order to rid the animals of the carrier ticks.

A large dip was constructed at San Julian, into which all of the cattle would regularly be driven and submerged in a concoction of water,

Cattle dipping to control diseases, about 1910.

carbolic acid, tobacco juices, and sulfur. The combination proved effective in controlling the spread of the disease. The dip was also used for ticks and scabbies on sheep and continued in use on San Julian until the 1930's. The gates at each end of the ranch road were kept closed. No cattle were allowed to pass through the ranch unless the owners were fairly certain that they were free of the disease. In this way they avoided contamination.

When Minnesota and Wisconsin passed legislation in the early 1920's to eliminate tuberculosis from their cattle, some dairy farmers took advantage of California's laxity and dumped many infected cattle into this state. The disease spread rapidly among the California herds, in not only dairy cattle but beef cattle as well. The result was a protracted and costly effort at identifying the infected cattle and their elimination.

On San Julian, the range cattle would be brought into fields near headquarters and run through a chute, where every adult animal was injected under the base of the tail and put out to pasture. They would be returned to the corral on the third day and put through the chute again in order for the veterinarian to feel in the area of the injection to see if there was swelling, an indication of a positive reaction. If there was swelling, the animal was marked with a large yellow chalk mark and would be consigned to the market for slaughter; infected parts were carefully eliminated.

We did not have many infected animals, but as long as there was even one, the whole herd had to be tested. The program took about five years and cost thousands of dollars before we were declared clean.

Bang's disease, which can cause sterility in bulls, is passed through the milk of infected animals and causes undulant fever in humans. Bang's disease can be spread by ticks carried by deer or by mucus from one bovine to another. It too was brought under control, but is endemic in areas of brush and ticks and is carried by deer.

Blackleg is also endemic and strikes calves in the spring when the grass is lush and the calves are between three and six months old. It is always customary for a rancher to vaccinate for blackleg when calves are young. Other diseases too, such as *anaplasmosis*, which causes anemia and often abortion, were finally controlled.

Leptospirosis is a disease prevalent in areas where animals have access to water contaminated by cattle. A spirochete multiplies in the ponds where cattle urinate, and a serious problem can occur in the livers of the cattle.

A disease caused by a fungus that is widespread over the ranges of California is known as *actinomycosis*. It enters the bloodstream through the mouth and tongue by way of wounds caused by sharp-pointed foxtail or rip-gut brome. The spore floats around in the bloodstream, finally settling in the lymph glands of the neck or throat. A lump rises, or a growth on the base of the tongue. This causes the tongue to harden, with the result that the animal has difficulty regurgitating its cud or swallowing the feed it has masticated. The animal gradually starves to death.

A treatment was discovered by the veterinary school at the University of Denver. They found that sodium iodide, injected directly into the bloodstream, will cause the lump to disappear in a few days. We became proficient in the administration of this medicine, although it was sometimes very difficult to find the artery in the neck of a big bull.

This treatment came too late to save a fine polled shorthorn bull that I had "trailed" out from the midwest in 1935 behind a small Chevy coupe. (Theoretically, I should not have been able to tow such a heavy bull in a trailer all that distance, but, since I did not know that it was unlikely that I could accomplish the journey, it came off all right.)

Alfalfa and Sudan Grass

Alfalfa. Roll that mellifluous word over your tongue a few times and you may realize how happy a bovine can be when the real thing rolls over and over its tongue as it chews its cud. *Al-fal-fa* in Arabic means "the best grass," and except for the lack of tiny hairs on the leaves, it would indeed be the best grass.

What can the lack of hairs on the leaves of a plant have to do with the quality of that plant? you might ask. It can make the difference between bloat and no bloat, for even the tiniest hairs on the leaf of a plant can tickle the innards of an animal and cause the gastric gases to be expelled. The lack of hairs on the leaves of alfalfa causes an accumulation of methane gas in the stomach, particularly if the plant is young and lush and slightly wet from dew. The rapid build-up of gas in a ruminant's stomach can cause great discomfort and even death by pressure of the gas against the heart.

There are several ways to relieve this condition. The first and quickest way is to insert the blade of a long knife or a Trocar into the stomach just forward of the hip bone on the animal's left side. This should not be done by anyone inexperienced in the procedure. The second method, which can also be dangerous to the animal's life, is to stick a small hose down its throat and into the stomach, which allows the gas to escape. I have used both methods more or less successfully—except that the animal I stuck with a hunting knife always had evidence of the wound on its side and never healed completely.

There was the case of a yearling steer that became a chronic bloater, bloating on almost anything it ate. We would put this animal in the squeeze chute and stick a small flexible hose down its throat until it reached the stomach, at which time the methane gas escaped through the hose.

One day I said to Joe Souza, my helper, "Go into the house and get a match."

"For what purpose?"

"To light the gas!"

He scoffed, but complied with my request and brought his wife and children to witness my humiliation when the gas failed to burn. However, I struck the match and applied it to the releasing gas. It immediately caught fire and burned for a couple of minutes with a steady blue flame, much to the amazement of the spectators.

Alfalfa had other drawbacks on our ranch, not the least of which was the depredation by deer and gophers. The latter can best be controlled when the fields are frequently flooded (not practical in areas where water is not cheap and abundant). But the deer came by the dozens in the night to feed on their favorite food.

An even more serious problem was caused by the presence of alfalfa. That was the introduction of the Egyptian alfalfa weevil. For decades, burr clover proliferated over nearly all of San Julian. In the mid-1920's we began to notice that the clover was diminishing in certain locations, notably the fields closest to the ranch house, where a particular short plant, as well as foxtail and rip-gut brome, intruded. We raised alfalfa for some fifteen years at Yridises and I noticed the diminution of clover on the hillside pastures in the backlands where it was once so prevalent. Then I noticed that something was eating the clover leaves.

I contacted the county farm advisor about the problem and he had one of the farm advisors, Warren Bendixon from Santa Maria, come out to see what was causing the depredation. He took his sweep out with him and caught a large number of insects in the clover patches; these he identified as the Egyptian alfalfa weevil. These weevils had migrated out to the hills from our alfalfa fields and were consuming the clover, the most important of our pasture grasses. (Being a legume, clover supplies nitrogen to the soil and furnishes protein to the cattle and, being high in phosphorus, clover promotes the appetite of animals when the feed becomes dry.) We immediately discontinued raising alfalfa. It has taken nearly twenty years for the weevil to die out so that the clover can again become an important part of our feed. Meanwhile, foxtail and rip-gut brome have become more prevalent. However, the clover is a tenacious and long-lived seed plant, and might come back.

Sudan grass is a very useful plant to cultivate; it is succulent and nutritious when it is grazed before it goes to seed and will often furnish heavy regrowth. But it, too, can cause a problem to cattle or sheep. The sugars of alkaloids in the plant will generally turn to hydrogen cyanide if the plant gets frosted or goes through a severe drought, and an animal eating the plant after that stage can very quickly die.

The sudan grass is a cane. That is, it has a solid stem, and this feature makes it difficult to bale unless it has been put through a crimper that allows the stem to dry out before the leaves lose all of their color and vitamins. Sudan was baled for many years at San Julian, but the bales nearly always molded on account of the high moisture in the stems. Although prolific in seed production, the plant will never reseed and has to be replanted each time it is raised. It is one of the highest yielding plants we can raise and graze. It does not yield as much as corn or sorghum, both of which have to be cultivated and cannot compete with the morning glory that infests our farming land.

Oil and Geology
and Thomas Dibblee

SHORTLY after the 1928 discovery of oil in the Luton-Bell field near Ellwood, a great deal of interest in the geology of the surrounding country became evident. We had friends in the East who, not knowing the distance or topography of the region, contacted us by telephone in order to determine if we had any information as to the geology of the ranch, and whether we would be interested in leasing a part or all of the land for oil exploration. Little geological study had been done on the ranch, which at that time consisted of 22,000 acres. The only study that had been done here was a cursory inspection and sort of field trip made by Dr. Bailey Willis when he came here to camp with a dozen or so Stanford students in 1918.

Wilson Dibblee hired Harry Johnson, a geologist from the Los Angeles area, to do a thorough geological study of the ranch. Johnson was a strapping six-footer with a moustache and red hair. He was probably in his early forties; a greater storyteller would be hard to find.

Tom, Wilson and Anita Oreña Dibblee's son, was a young fellow in high school the summer Johnson spent doing field work, and young Tom followed Johnson all over the ranch on foot studying geologic structures,

Thomas W. Dibblee, Jr., eminent geologist

taking samples of rocks, and estimating the dip of the structures. They tried to find faults that would indicate the closure of an anticline, or a dip in the anticline that might indicate hydrocarbons were trapped in such a structure. Several promising anticlines were found, especially on Los Palos Colorados (one of the northwestern parcels). It had been agreed by all members of the family that if oil in paying quantities were found on anyone's property, it would be shared by all. (This was only a gentleman's agreement, and there was no written record, so the agreement is no longer in effect.)

Further study of the structures determined that there was no closure of the large anticlines, meaning chances were slim that any hydrocarbons remained within those areas. Over the years we have had several leases for oil exploration on the various ranches, and two wells have been drilled on the property, all with negative results. Several wells have been drilled on land adjacent to ours, also with poor showings. One well over the hill near the river came up with showings of oil in a small lens of sand. Joe Hollister, a geologist from the neighboring ranch, declared there might be thin lenses or stratographic traps of oil that could be in "fingers" from the offshore structures. Hollister advised me that if any oil companies came around to lease, we should never insist

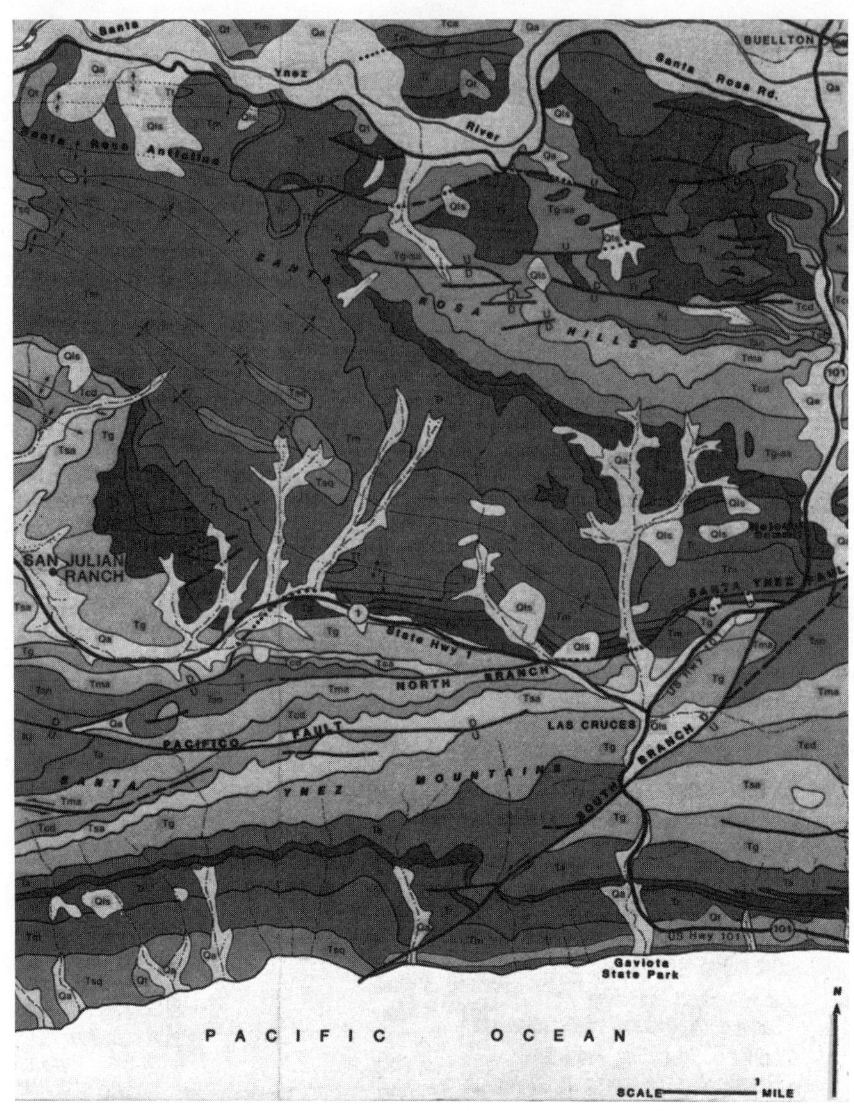

Tom Dibblee's map of the San Julian area,
showing the many geological formations on the ranch.

162

that they drill; in that way they would never know whether or not there was oil. He doubted there was oil, and so far we have taken his advice.

Two wells were drilled on San Julian. The first was drilled by Texaco on Panchita Summers' Las Ytias; it went down several thousand feet only to hit the cretaceous formation. This seems to be an artificial boundary beyond which oil companies do not drill because cretaceous sands are so tight they are likely to have little porosity in which hydrocarbons can move.

Tom Dibblee became interested in geology and went on to Stanford University, where he took a course in that science. Soon after college he obtained a job with Union Oil Company. After several years with Union, he was hired by Richfield Oil Company, an offshoot of the Barnsdall and Rio Grande Oil companies that had done so well at Ellwood; it is now part of Atlantic-Richfield (ARCO) oil company.

Tom was sent to do a geological study of Cuyama, and later went to do other work for the company. Sometime in the 1940's, Norris Oil, a Los Angeles firm, obtained a small lease on a portion of the Cuyama Ranch and came up with a fairly good well of high gravity. This brought all the oil companies scurrying to see what they could get in the way of leases. Richfield, which had the only comprehensive geological study of the region, called Tom Dibblee for his recommendations of what areas of the ranch were most favorable for oil. He outlined the places where he thought the best chance would be for oil, and so Richfield was able to lease the likely acreage while the others simply did not know where to look. The result was that Richfield, then in bad financial straits, hit huge quantities of oil, enabling the company to extricate itself from its financial difficulties and become one of the leading oil companies in the country.

A sideline to this story is that the Cebrians of San Francisco, the previous owners of the ranch, had failed to file in San Luis Obispo a deed that Mr. Cebrian had made out to one of his children, transferring the subsurface rights to the land. When the brothers Hub and Joe Russell, cousins of C.E. Russell of San Julian [see "The Men of San Julian"], were negotiating to buy the property before the discovery of

Yvonne Dibblee Donohoe (left) and Virginia Dibblee, Tom Dibblee's sisters.

oil, a search of the deeds to the ranch was made and it was determined that no mention of any oil or subsurface rights were recorded. This meant that the rights to such minerals or oil would go with the land, and so the Russell brothers were the recipients of huge royalties resulting from the strike.

After many years of oil geology, Tom Dibblee went to work for the United States Geological Survey. He started mapping the geology of the many California faults, concentrating mainly on the San Andreas fault. He worked for the Geological Survey for many years and did extensive mapping in many parts of the state. In fact, he has done so much geological mapping that he is considered the most prolific geological mapper in the world. His maps are models of accuracy and clarity.

I had a friend who had once been an oil geologist, but who had retired from oil geology and gone into water geology. I asked the fellow, Bob Williams, how he happened to be such a good water finder. "I find water mainly with the help of Tom Dibblee's geological maps."

John Curran, a geologist friend of Tom's from Santa Barbara, recognized the value of Dibblee's maps and the benefits that could be derived from the publication and dissemination of those maps. Together, they and some others organized the Thomas W. Dibblee Foundation to publish the many geological maps Tom had drawn. A process of coloring the maps in order to show more easily the geological features was perfected, and the myriad maps are in the process of being published.

Tom Dibblee has received numerous awards and great recognition for the valuable contribution he has made to the science of geology, including a presidential award from President Ronald Reagan. His renown is worldwide, and he can enjoy the satisfaction of having been appreciated for his work during his lifetime, a recognition few people receive.

Diatomaceous Earth

THE DISCOVERY and development of diatomaceous earth (or DE, as we call it) in the Lompoc Valley started in 1893 when the Francis Baalam family of Lompoc, who farmed the San Miguelito Canyon area south of town, started quarrying the substance and selling it in brick form or bags as insulating material.

The venture was not profitable. A brewer from Milwaukee named Kriger somehow got the idea that the substance could be used as a filter for his beer. In 1904, Kriger interested two Germans, R.J. Wig and a Mr. Fitka, to process the material. This proved feasible and a small factory was built to process the material. Some of the diatomaceous earth (known as Kieselguhr to Germans) was sold as insulation.

The insulating and filtration properties of diatomaceous earth are due to the large numbers of microscopic diatoms that compose the material. These diatoms are marine organisms that lived in the cold inland seas millions of years ago. It is my theory (unbacked by scientific evidence) that the proliferation of the diatoms in this prehistoric sea was promoted by Tranquillion, a volcano in the area. Tranquillion spewed chemicals such as phosphates into the surrounding area, making a brew that encouraged a rapid and voluminous growth of diatoms. These settled to the bottom of the ocean when they died and formed large deposits of the

Diatomaceous earth mine at Palos Colorados on Rancho San Julian, looking south-west. San Julian Valley can be seen in the upper left, with the Pacific Ocean beyond.

substance, unaffected by the tides or ocean currents. When the land gradually rose out of the sea, much of the exposed diatomite must have then been eroded away, since it is very light and subject to wind and rain. Portions that exist today must have been capped by layers of limestone, sandstone, or chert, which has protected them from the elements over the eons.

When the Baalams started their venture selling bricks and powder for insulation, little did they realize that the property would eventually produce billions of tons of a usable and highly profitable product.

In the mid-1920's, when the German I.G. Farbenindustries, commenced their large-scale production of chemicals, they started a great

The DE mine on Rancho San Julian

demand for the filtration products of DE and the Johns-Manville Company took over the lease in order to finance the new technology.

In 1936, a splinter group from Johns-Manville started a rival company, Starr Quaries, to quarry the DE from the nearby hills on the Larsons' property; another quarry on the Palos Verdes Peninsula, southwest of Los Angeles, was opened about the same time. A manufactory to process the material was erected at Walteria, near today's Torrance.

In 1940, Starr Quarries acquired a lease to mine diatomaceous earth on the Palos Colorados tract of Rancho San Julian, then owned by William Dibblee. Shortly thereafter, this lease, together with the Starr lease on the Larson property, was acquired by Great Lakes Carbon Corporation, a large company from Chicago. This concern was owned by the Shakel family (Ethel Shakel married Robert Kennedy). They were able to furnish large amounts of money to promote the quarrying on the San Julian property.

On the Los Yridises tract, which is about two miles east of the Palos Colorados deposit, the beds of chert, which were once diatomite but metamorphosed by heat and pressure into hard silica, lie in beds trending east and west in alternating synclines and anticlines. Small areas of diatomite are interspersed between the folds in the earth.

Quarrying on a grand scale soon commenced in a large syncline on the northern boundary of the property, near the Cooper ranch in the Santa Ynez Valley. The material was hauled by truck to the plant at Walteria. This continued until 1952, when a plant was built at the junction of highways 246 and 1 (we call Highway 1 the San Julian Road). In 1958, environmental concerns about dust, noise, and traffic in Palos Verdes, as well as the Portuguese Bend landslide, caused the closure of that quarry

The only lake on the ranch was created when diatomaceous earth was quarried from this deposit on Los Palos Colorados from 1942 to 1962. The surface area of the lake is about ten acres.

and the dismantling of the plant at Walteria, which was moved and added to the plant in Lompoc. The production of DE from the quarry in Miguelito Canyon and on San Julian increased.

In 1966, George Shakel and his brother were killed in an airplane crash in California and, as a result, the majority of the leases near Lompoc were acquired by General Refractories Company, a Philadelphia firm producing refractory bricks for the smelting of metals. The large syncline at Palos Colorados had gotten quite deep by that time and the wet DE at that great depth became heavily carbonaceous and too costly to process; the carbonaceous material would have to be burned away using excessive amounts of fuel.

An intensive program of drilling on half of the 2,800 acres of land determined the extent and quality of the DE in the remainder of the property. The results were encouraging, although the deposits were not as concentrated as in the large quarries. The beds of DE and interspersed overburden were more convoluted and a different method was employed to lift the material. They now use front-end loaders that lift the material from benches comprising up to twenty feet of material. As the beds of DE and interspersed overburden lie at angles of between 30 and 60 degrees to the horizontal, it is easy to outline the areas of good or poor DE as well as to separate them for stockpiling or disposal into dumps.

Processing diatomaceous earth consists of passing the material over screens to eliminate any rock. The product is then ground and burned in a kiln to remove moisture and process the DE into sizes that will meet the specifications of the orders received. Heating DE causes a coalescing of the fine particles to obtain larger ones to meet the flow-rate specifications; soda ash or some other substance is occasionally added to obtain a different flow rate.

The Johns-Manville deposit, now called Manville Corporation, is very extensive and probably will last many years. The deposit on San Julian has perhaps another twenty-five years.

RICHARD BOND

ONE OF my oldest friends to whom I wish to pay tribute for the breadth and depth of his knowledge of nature and our surroundings, and his willingness to impart his knowledge to us lesser mortals, is Richard Bond of Santa Barbara.

Dick Bond was born in New York City, the son of Marshall and Amy Bond. The senior Bond led an exciting life as an explorer and gold hunter, as recounted by his son, Marshall Bond, Jr., in his book, *Gold Hunter*. Marshall, Sr., was the son of a prominent New York State judge. All male members of that family were Yalies, including Dick and Marshall Bond, Jr.

I first became acquainted with Dick and Marshall when, at the age of eight years, I attended the Hicks School on the first block of East Arrellaga Street in Santa Barbara. It was run by Rodney Heggie, a fine gentleman.

My experiences at that school were somewhat bizarre, I confess, including the time I told my mother that my teacher, Mr. Tupper, had kicked me, which was promptly reported to the headmaster who, of course, disproved the incident as a figment of my imagination. On another occasion, I became so enthralled with a paving gang doing their job a block from school that I stopped to watch the goings-on—until I was discovered by scouts from the school, who knew where to look for an errant little boy with a pump wagon.

After graduating from Hicks, Dick went on to St. Paul's School in Concord, New Hampshire, and then Yale, as did his brother Marshall. There, Dick became interested in botany, biology, ornithology, herpatology, zoology, ichthyology, and other natural sciences. I believe he remembered everything he was ever taught, and he was never reluctant to impart any of his broad knowledge to his many friends and admirers.

I once told Dick about my great-grandfather, Dr. Joseph Henry Poett, who, after his second wife died, returned to Europe. When Dr. Poett died, he was buried at Dinard, near San Malo, France. After many years, it was decided to have his remains brought back to San Francisco, where they were interred in Golden Gate Cemetery. The State of California decided to build a freeway through that cemetery, and it was necessary to reinter the remains, which were taken to a family plot in San Mateo. During the third interment, it was noted that the casket was very heavy, and our cousin Josephine Stetson, a granddaughter by the second marriage, decided to have the casket opened. To the great astonishment of all the viewers, it was seen that the body had become petrified. When I mentioned this to Dick Bond, he said, "It is well known that the mineral springs in the neighborhood of Dinard can cause such a phenomenon."

He knew about so many things that none of his many friends were surprised when he came up with such an answer.

Dick told me why the army worms did so much damage to the beans in the large Oxnard plain. All of the trees had been cut away to make room for farming, and the blackbirds, which ordinarily would have kept the moth of that worm under control, had no place to roost. He said not to worry about the oak moth, which ate the leaves of the local oak trees, because they would soon be diminished by the microscopic wasp, which would eat the larvae of the moth and cause the invasion to quickly die out, which of course happened just as he had predicted.

He knew every plant, bird, animal, and insect that existed in the neighborhood, and could describe their habits and place of origin. In short, Dick was a walking encyclopedia of nature, and I never tired of listening to his description of natural things.

A calf finds a cozy spot between two old sycamore trees on Los Yridises.

He was the first professional "ecologist" I ever knew, and he made me cognizant of the ways of nature. Dick would go up onto the hills of our farming fields and show us where erosion was taking its toll by pointing out that finger erosion, which by its nature is visible only to those who know what to look for, had occurred when fine grains of silt were washed away and coarser grains then revealed. "Come down to the creek and I will show you where this soil has been deposited." Sure enough, when we went down to the creek, we found that most of the pools we used to fish in had been filled with silt. It took considerable persuasion on my part to convince Wilson Dibblee to get the tenants to farm the hillsides on the contours. Eventually we had to give up farming the steep hills when rills and gullies from the erosion became more evident. Many of the farmers resented the interference caused by these observations, yet the viability of the land depended on the retirement of hillside farming.

Dick Bond became a consulting biologist to the Santa Barbara County Soil Conservation District and was responsible for the introduction of the beaver into our area. He said the beaver or some other type of animal had probably been instrumental in building the alluvial deposit in the valley, and that the beaver might, over a long period of time, help to restore the deep arroyo into a more natural form. Of course, in the millions of years it took to build up the alluvium, there were no cattle or humans to upset the balance of nature.

Dick was later transferred to the Virgin Islands, where he took his wife and young daughter. After several years at San Croix, he divorced his wife and married a native of French Haiti, who bore him several black children. He was a heavy smoker and contracted cancer of the lungs; he came back to Santa Barbara for an operation and recuperation, and then returned to the islands.

Dick heard there was an opening for a curator of the Santa Barbara Museum of Natural History and applied for that position, but was refused the appointment because of his black wife. Dick had been assistant curator at a museum in Cairo shortly after his graduation from Yale and would have made a fine choice for Santa Barbara.

Like many geniuses (and I consider him to have been one), Dick Bond was a great egotist as well as self-proclaimed atheist.

In later years, after recurring bouts with cancer, Dick converted to Christianity. He died in the late 1970's, and we all miss his valuable advice. So, "*Ojalá, y vaya con Dios*, Dick Bond."

Others in the field of soil conservation who deserve mention are Clarence Blakeboro, now of Santa Barbara, and Earl Ross of Lompoc, both of whom came when the Civilian Conservation Corps came to Lompoc. Also Nelson Rutherford, and last but not least, Max Wilson, who devoted so many years to the cause of conservation.

TRAMPS

FOR as long as I can remember, hardly a day passed at San Julian when we did not have a visit from one or more of the "kings of the road." I presume there were more of these fellows who followed the railroad tracks that went through the Hollister Ranch.

By some mysterious sign language or code, these tramps always seemed to know what sort of treatment they would receive at the next habitation. Chalk marks on the bridges indicated how far and exactly what they would have to do to receive a handout. No tramp was ever turned away from San Julian without a meal, provided he (there were never women tramps) would do a certain amount of work for a good square meal, which had to be performed before he was fed.

There was a large woodshed near the kitchen in which was stored a good number of logs cut to stove length, and the tramp was required to split and carry into the kitchen enough wood to fill a large wood box near the stove, or, if the box was full, he would be required to split an extra amount of wood. The stove was a large iron range, with two ovens, about six feet long; a steady fire kept the room and food warm.

The Chinese cook allowed the tramps to eat their meals at the kitchen table, ever watchful that they did not try to get away with anything. Whenever any ornery or reluctant character appeared to get out of hand or demand food before or without some work, the cook would brandish

Entrance to the kitchen and working men's dining room at Casa San Julian. The bell on the roof called the men for meals.

a huge carving knife or whistle for one of the dogs, which would help keep the man in line. Once a tramp came to my mother's door as she was putting out some scraps for the dog. He was so famished that he immediately gobbled down the leftovers. How we laughed to see the expression in the puzzled dog's eyes—as well as the satisfaction of the poor hungry tramp.

These fellows invariably carried a bedroll on their back or over one shoulder and often slept under the bridges. Sometimes, if the weather was inclement or very cold, they would ask to sleep in the barn, where they would curl up on a pile of hay or straw and keep warm by the presence of the horses. Each one who was allowed to sleep in the barn was made to promise not to smoke in the barn. The saddlehorse barn once burned down from a fire caused by a careless tramp.

On the whole, the tramps were a decent lot, although almost always dirty, and generally not very loquacious. Most of them were drifters with no specific goal in mind. Just "on the go." And there were hardly ever any foreigners in the lot. They usually smoked roll-your-own cigarettes or chewed tobacco, and were invariably bearded or in need of a shave. Tramp traffic continued until the early 1930's, when the county constructed the road across the creek away from the ranch house.

Rancho San Julian:
Recollections

RECOLLECTIONS

I.

MY EARLIEST recollections of San Julian are from the time that we went camping there in the summer of 1914, shortly before the outbreak of the first World War.

We pitched a large tent under a huge sycamore tree near a flowing stream. Above our camp, the canyon was steep and narrow. A sack dam across the creek impounded the water, which was piped to our tent. From there it flowed beyond to an open wooden flume that carried water to a large wooden tank above the vegetable garden near the Casa, the main ranch house. Our camp was about a quarter of a mile upstream from the Casa, and about a hundred feet higher in elevation.

The wooden flume was open, supported by a wooden trestle that kept it out of the reach of rodents and cattle. The water for the Casa came from a separate source, a spring about a mile away in a place aptly named Water Canyon.

We had a large wood stove in the tent, fueled by fallen branches of oak, sycamore, and willow. The sycamore and willow wood imparted such an exotic aroma that the smell of these burning woods takes me back to the carefree days of that pleasant year.

We camped out instead of using the Casa because all of the family was coming to the ranch that year, and there would not be room in the big

Frederica (right), Mercedes 'Nan,' and Dibblee Poett,
around 1915. Their brother Harold was born later.

house for five Poetts. It was a lark to which we all looked forward—
except perhaps by Mother, who knew better than we the hardships to be
encountered. But she was a good sport and took it all in stride. We slept
on spring cots, which we frequently moved outside to sleep under the
stars, and we were generally up at the first light of dawn.

The large overhanging sycamore tree under which our tent was
pitched shed a fine, fuzzy down from its leaves beginning about the first
of August. This dust caused a great deal of sneezing, and that is why we
called it Sneeze Canyon.

The weather that summer was pleasant and balmy. We roamed the
hills and valleys searching for caves, and climbed countless trees, both

oak and sycamore, without a single fall. We watched the sheep shearers do their work, which seemed so glamorous to us, and even got inside the huge, burlap wool-bags to tamp the wool tight in the sack. Most of the time, my sister Nan and I went barefoot. We formed callouses on our feet that enabled us to go almost any place, except the patches of Tecelote thistles, which have long sharp spines that can penetrate through the tops of tennis shoes and are really wicked.

There seemed to be no restrictions on our wanderings and we went wherever we felt like, except that we were required to be home for meals. As we had not yet learned to read the sun, we generally got home in plenty of time. We were lucky, too, that we never stepped on boards with nails protruding, as we might have gotten a puncture wound and the tetanus that often follows such an occurrence. Nor did we have any close encounters with rattlesnakes, which always seemed to show up in the most unlikely places; the rattlers in our region do not get up in the trees as they do in the pine forests.

Not far from our camp, on the road to El Cielito, was the grave of an Indian, Andres, who had worked on San Julian, and whose resting place was fenced off and tended by Alfredo Espinosa, who used to go there occasionally to pay his respects to his old friend. Close by this grave on a wide bench of the hillside is located a "chipping field" where the Indians used to bring chert rocks to make into arrows or spearheads. One can still find these artifacts, especially after a rain, when some of the topsoil is washed away.

That pleasant summer passed much too quickly and we looked forward to the following year when we would again enjoy the freedom of the ranch. This, however, was not to be. Harry Poett and his wife asked us to visit them in Hillsborough and take in San Francisco's Panama-Pacific International Exposition, celebrating the completion of the Panama Canal. The following year, we invited Harry and his two children to visit us at San Julian. We took Evelyn and Harry riding over a great part of the ranch and taught them to ride bareback. We had to ride double, as my sisters and I were each allowed to have a horse.

Frederica had a good buckskin gelding, Nan was given the use of Aunt Carmen's bay thoroughbred mare (which could also pull a cart or buggy), and I had the use of a handsome sorrel gelding named Blandy. A wire cut on his leg just above the hoof caused Blandy to stumble; the *vaqueros* were leery of him on that account. But with my light weight and no saddle to carry, as Nan and I rode bareback most of the time, he seldom stumbled with me. Frederica always used an English saddle; the stirrups would disengage in the event of a fall or the saddle turning.

Blandy always limped going away from home, but, as his ankle became more supple with use, he got over the lameness. Whenever we would stop, whether to open a gate or fix a broken wire, Blandy turned toward home and his desire to return became a matter of great concern. When we reached our destination, his impatience knew no bounds, and his return trip was a matter of prancing and throwing his head in the most vigorous manner until he was allowed to gallop and challenge any horse that got ahead of him. Once when we were driving cattle on Los Palos Colorados, the cattle stirred up a nest of yellow jackets that attacked the horses. I slipped off Blandy and started running for a clump of brambles. Looking back I saw my horse coming after me in hopes that I would rid him of the attackers. I started running around the clump, which was about twenty feet in diameter, but he was catching up to me, so I made a great leap and landed in the middle of the briars—to the great amusement of all watching this strange performance.

The head *vaquero* at San Julian was Santiago "Jim" Rios, who had been working on the ranch since 1885, when Ezequiel Ortega was a cattle boss here. Jim took over the job about ten years later. Jim was an expert with the *reata*, and used one about forty feet long. All the riders made their own *reatas* from the rawhide of cattle that had been killed for beef or had died on the range. Whenever a rider found a dead cow, it would be skinned and the hide salted; the price of rawhide was worth more than the labor of skinning them.

To make a *reata*, a man would cut a narrow strip of rawhide about three-eighths of an inch wide and about the length of the desired *reata* plus about ten extra feet. These strips were then stretched to straighten and covered with tallow to make them more supple. The hair would be scraped off the strip and three or four more strips of equal length

Augustín Rios, Jim's son, with a rawhide reata.

and width would be stretched alongside. When the rawhide was deemed straight and supple enough to be braided, the work of braiding and stretching the forming *reata* would begin. Before the braiding was begun, the strips would be placed in a vat or water trough to soften the leather. Sometimes *reatas* were made with six strands, but usually four, and the woven rope would then be greased again with tallow. These braided rawhide ropes were truly a work of art and, if properly cared for, would last many years.

Jim Rios was probably the best cattle boss we ever had. He was gentle with the cattle, but a bit hard on his horse. The ones he rode always seemed to have saddle sores, whether from the saddle or his habit of trotting his horse most of the time, I do not know. He knew the cattle and they knew him so well that very few were wild. He seldom chased an animal if he could avoid it. Occasionally a cow would have to be lassoed out on the range. I have seen Jim rope and knock a cow down by quickly riding his horse around and around the animal so that its legs became tangled up and it would collapse. After the animal was treated, a foxtail removed from its eye or a lump on the jaw lanced, the difficult job would be to get the rope off its head or horns and get away without being chased by the animal. Like a good cowboy, Jim Rios trained his horse to hold the animal while he treated it. Often the cow would be mad enough to challenge the rider, but Jim generally dissuaded the beast with his quirt if it got too close.

Jim rode the fences, took care of the troughs, checked the cattle, and watched for strays that sometimes came in from our neighbors' pastures. He conferred daily with the *patrón* or *mayordomo* as to conditions of the feed, cattle, fences, or troughs. He taught us much about the ranch and told tales of the old days and the men who had worked on the ranch. He told us of good and bad years and of the horses he had ridden.

Most of the riders did not care to ride mares or fillies, preferring the males. I was never able to figure the reason for this preference, since I had just as good, if not better, luck with mares as with geldings—with one exception. I was never able to shoot from a mare, but I had a gelding that would not even flinch when I shot from the saddle. We had a horse at Yridises that was so hard-mouthed that one could hardly stop the beast. He was tough, too. He would start off at a gallop and go at that pace nearly all the way up to Rosa.

The highest point on our ranch, Rosa has a geodetic monument designating its altitude (1,773 feet). From there one can overlook much of the Santa Ynez Valley. It was from a place near there that I used to get a big kick out of rolling huge rocks down onto our neighbor's land. They bounced and gyrated as they leaped into the air on their one-mile plunge toward the bottom of the valley. When the neighbor finally complained, I had to desist from the enjoyable pursuit. I don't blame him at all.

In the early days on San Julian, there was a hay stacker that was used to stack the loose hay brought in by means of buck rakes, pulled by two

Frances Summers (left) and Dibblee Summers, children of Francisca and William T. Summers, spent many summers at the ranch.

horses. When two or three shocks of hay were on the forks of the stacker, the team of horses hitched to a cable would be urged forward at a fast pace to raise the load by means of cables and pulleys on the high parts of the machine. The hay would go up and fall onto the middle of the stack and then be forked around by two men to keep the stack level. These men used to ride up on top of the hay and jump off just as the hay was tossed off by the loader, landing on the stack.

Our cousin Frances Summers decided that she, too, could accomplish this dangerous leap, despite the foreman's warning. Well, she got on the loader and rode it up, but failed to jump at the proper time. She fell to the ground, hitting her head on a cable, which knocked her out for about fifteen minutes. We were scared that she was going to die, but she seemed to recover. I think that Frances's subsequent headaches were a result of the fall.

We would climb up onto a stack by means of ropes let down by the workers and enjoyed tumbling over the stack, which was springy and fun to play on. After they had been peaked somewhat, the large stacks were covered with tarpaulins. A fence, sometimes consisting of stout boards, then was built around it so that the loose hay could easily be pitched down to the cattle, which could feed without actually getting into the stack. Loose hay, however, was inconvenient to handle, and we finally ended up using only baled hay. Another drawback to storing loose hay is the damage done to the hay by mice, which make a good home in the usually dry and warm stack and thrive on the grain thus obtained.

Most of our riding horses were standard bred (sometimes called American saddlebred). We purchased these from the Hollisters, who had a good stallion of that breed. Occasionally we used the services of a fine Arabian stallion belonging to Adolfo Camarillo of Ventura County, and we got some good horses from the cross, somewhat larger than the Arabians but with the renowned stamina of the Arabians. We also got a few palominos, which, of course, are not a breed but simply a color. A great effort was put into establishing a breed of palominos but without very much success—as Dwight Murphy found out after many years of trying to establish one. Only about one in seven of the colts thus produced came out the color desired.

When the quarterhorse came into prominence—in the early 1940's, I believe—it became necessary to purchase new saddles with double rigging. As the early quarterhorses were built like a barrel without any withers, or with very low ones, we often had to add a breast-strap and britchen, which went over the rump of the horse to keep the saddle from sliding over its neck. For corral work and parting, the quarterhorse has the advantage over many other breeds as it is agile and short-coupled, but I do not think that the breed has the stamina of the thoroughbred when it comes to long days of riding or the speed at long distances. Admittedly, the thoroughbred is high-strung and thin-skinned (therefore subject to more infestation by ticks and cuts from wires and sharp sticks). Eddie Vail, late of Santa Rosa Island, used to say, however, that he got by with about two-thirds as many thoroughbreds as with any other breed of horse.

San Julian seems to have gotten steeper as I grew older, and one day as I was riding down a steep Yridises canyon on my trusty Arabian mare, Paloma, she stumbled and went down on her knees. I fell off over her head and rolled about forty feet down to the creek bottom. After recovering my bearings, I looked around and to my amazement saw a huge boulder with a fossil bone protruding, nearly like the one on the hill just above. But that large stone remains in the creek bottom, which is too difficult a place to build a road with our present equipment, and will probably remain there for some time, despite the probability that it might sell for a thousand dollars or more.

Paloma waited for me where she had stumbled, and I scrambled back up the bank on all fours like a bear.

Speaking of Bears

William Heath Davis, in his book, *Seventy-Five Years in California*, recounted how one of the Carrillos living in Monterey County was chasing a bear, Carrillo on horseback. Suddenly the bear disappeared from view, having fallen into a gulch that was hidden by the tall grass. In a few seconds the horse and rider joined the animal at the bottom of the ravine. Scrambling to get away from an unpleasant encounter, the bear started to climb the bank, and the rider, also wishing to have the bear at a distance, gave the animal a push on his haunch to help him out and avoid a potentially lethal encounter. There is little doubt that each of the participants of this episode was relieved when the bear departed.

Dario Oreña (son of María Antonia de la Guerra and Gaspar Oreña) told of a bull that was fed some poison—probably arsenic—and turned loose, with the expectation that he would die and be bait for some bears that were killing cattle. The bull survived the poison and returned to headquarters about a week later without a hair on his body, but otherwise seemingly healthy.

Alfred Robinson, in *Life in California*, tells of a trick someone played on him. He and some friends went camping not far from the sea, where there was a *matanza*, or killing ground, where the ranchers would bring their cattle to be slaughtered for the hides and tallow. Nearby was a tent in which Robinson was to sleep. When he retired for the night, he heard all sorts of menacing noises and looked to see what was going on. Dozens of menacing grizzly bears milled about outside, seemingly full of beef—and therefore with no care to attack a man, a fact of which Robinson was not aware. Needless to say, Robinson did not sleep very soundly that night, and his friends had a great laugh at his expense.

Two biologists reported in the *Los Angeles Times* several years ago that there were once at least ten thousand grizzly bears in California—probably in the 1820's and 1830's, when the large *matanzas* (slaughters) were in progress. All that good beef left around to eat without even having to kill the cattle. The result was that between periods of slaughtering, the bears preyed on the range cattle, which could not escape the bears as easily as could wild animals. The situation between the bears and the Indians was at a standoff. The Indians' arrows could not ordinarily kill a bear, but the bear respected the Indians and did not molest them too much—until the bears found the free meals of slaughtered beef and quickly multiplied. It was not until the *gringos* came with their Winchester repeating rifles that the grizzly was finally eliminated. Bears were too fond of beef to suit the *gringos*.

The native Californians, too, had been killing the grizzlies since the days of the *matanza's* end, but the ball of the Spaniard's musket did not strike the bear hard enough or penetrate its thick hide as did the bullet of the Winchester rifle. The cruel sport of the bull-and-bear fight became popular when the Californians learned that with a good strong horse, a rider could lasso a bear and bring it home. The bear was placed in a small corral or enclosure into which a big powerful bull was led. The fight would last to the death, with the bull often the winner. This sadistic sport continued until nearly the end of the last century. Harry Hollister used to recount with great glee about the bear-and-bull fights he had witnessed. The bear always ended up dead, whether by the bull or the rancher's rifle. Strangely, no bear skins have survived, at least not on our ranch, though there must have been many of them killed.

Letters from Joaquin and Francisco de la Guerra often mention that bears were killing cattle on San Julian or Simi in the 1860's and 1870's. Once a bear had tasted beef, there was no stopping it from killing cattle unless it was killed. I have not read any accounts of grizzlies killing sheep, although I cannot deny that such events occurred. Perhaps this was due to the fact that the sheep were tended by a herder during the day, and the bear might not have desired to tangle with the shepherd and his dog. At night, on San Julian, the sheep were enclosed in corrals surrounded by heavy barriers of oak or other tree trimmings, through which it would be very difficult for a bear to climb.

I have never seen or heard mention of wolves; the worst enemy the sheep might encounter would be a coyote, but these animals usually stayed out of range of the shepherd's dog, and seldom killed sheep tended by a shepherd. The gates of the sheep corrals were generally made of stout boards and were usually high enough (perhaps seven feet high) to prevent any animal from jumping over.

Where the sheep and cattle grazed, we often sought the meadow mushrooms. We were always very careful to assure that the mushrooms were of the right color and shape and did not grow under a tree. Long observation has shown me that the mushroom will not grow until the cold weather and rain come at the proper time.

When the weather warms in the late winter or early spring, the meadow mushrooms and the yellow chantrelles cease to sprout. The chantrelle needs a heavy rain preceding the winter rains by about a month to really amount to anything, but this type of mushroom thrives on our land under the oak trees or brush, where nothing but mushrooms will grow on account of the acid left by the leaves of *Baccharis*. No grass or weeds will grow there, with the exception of the yerba buena, and perhaps a little stipa.

The chantrelles grow profusely along the cattle trails, where they are nourished by the cattle droppings, but they also grow on the steeper hillsides where the sun does not strike until late in the day or not at all. The chantrelles, which we ate until recently, are not, in my opinion, as tasty as the meadow mushroom.

II.

MY FATHER, Fred Poett, whom we called "D," was not a big man, but what he lacked in size he made up in courage and wit. One day we children were down by the blacksmith shop, where there were five or six men standing around talking, when one of them, a burly fellow named Plymer, started swearing.

My father said to him, "Plymer, I have repeatedly told you not to swear in the presence of women and children," whereupon Plymer picked up a large maul, or sledgehammer, and advanced menacingly toward my father. Dad suddenly leaped forward and struck him on the nose, causing Plymer to drop the maul.

Dad contemptuously cast aside the maul and said, "Plymer, you are fired. Come up to the office and get your check." And to Alejandro Pico he said, "Alex, hitch the bay mare to the buggy and take this fellow to Las Cruces. He is to be off the ranch within an hour."

Needless to say, there was no more foul language in our presence, and the incident was the topic of conversation for many days.

"How did Mr. Poett strike that fellow so quickly?"

"What a lot of guts he has to take on a bully with that big hammer."

My dad was a good rider, and I never saw him unhorsed, but he had a habit of flapping his arms as his horse cantered, so that he looked like a bird about to take wing. He owned a horse that had a bad habit of pulling back and breaking every rope with which he was tied, so "D" said, "I'll fix you." He took the horse down to the large *barranca* below the house and tied it to a stout willow tree on a sandy bank near a deep pool. When the horse pulled back and broke the rope, its momentum carried it back and it fell over the bank into the pool. A couple of rounds of this, and the horse decided that it had had enough of pulling back.

As my dad was courting my mother in Santa Barbara, she had another suitor, an Italian count. He was an excellent rider, and my dad figured out a strategy to eliminate his rival. He challenged the fellow to a horse race. The Italian readily agreed, since he had a fine thoroughbred stallion he believed could easily outdistance the nondescript horse my dad had.

The race was held on what is now West Cabrillo Boulevard and began at the foot of State Street, near the entrance to Stearns Wharf. A shot was fired to signal the start of the race, and they were off in a cloud of dust. Fred Poett quickly opened his early lead. He weighed less than one hundred and fifty pounds; the foreigner, who was over six feet tall, weighed over two hundred pounds. Fred's horse had a large advantage in weight. Most of the spectators had bet on the count and his fine-looking steed, and as Fred Poett turned the corner leading to what is now Pershing Park he glanced to see his rival about eight lengths behind. Crossing the finish line he quickly reined in his horse and vaulted to the ground to greet his rival. At this, the other suitor's stallion came to an abrupt halt, throwing its rider to the ground in a most unceremonious manner. The assembled spectators jeered, and the Italian count quickly disappeared from the scene of his ignominy. This story generally has been embellished in the telling.

Fred Poett once asked his friend, Alex Center of San Francisco, to ship a horse of Fred's down by boat. When the steamer arrived it was quickly discovered that Center had made an error. Dad telegraphed back to him: "You sent the wrong horse. I am sending this one back by the same boat." But the ship returned by way of the Hawaiian Islands; it is presumed that the horse had a fine sea voyage. The trip must have been calm, for if a horse gets seasick, it will most certainly die, as seasick horses cannot regurgitate.

The automobile was coming into use shortly after the turn of the century and my dad and his friend Charles Howard heard that there were two auto agencies up for bid. One was the Buick and the other the Krit. The Krit? What was that? The two agreed to toss to see who got the Buick.

Charles Howard was the lucky one. He became a millionaire, and was the owner of Sea-Biscuit, the fabulous stallion of the early 1940's. Howard's second wife was Manuela Hudson of the Hartnell clan from Monterey, a cousin of ours and a great beauty, who I had met at one of Santa Barbara's early fiestas. She later divorced Howard and married Alfred Vanderbilt.

My dad took the Krit agency. He used to go around the county and other parts of the state trying to interest people in the strange three-cylinder auto. His sales amounted to three or four cars per year; he gave up on this maverick after a while.

My father's remarkable memory, not only for people but events, numbers, and trivia, came into evidence once while we were visiting our cousins in Hillsborough in 1915. His brother Harry had a safe that had belonged to their father, Alfred Poett, and Uncle Harry had lost the combination. Harry asked my dad if he could open it. Not letting on that he remembered the combination from ten or fifteen years before, my dad said that yes, he thought he might be able to open it. But first he would need some fine sandpaper or emery cloth and a stethoscope. Young Harry Poett was agog as my dad proceeded to sand his thumb and forefinger in preparation to open the safe. Then he put on the stethoscope and held it to the lock of the safe. Slowly turning the dial, Dad would say, ''Ah, I think I have it,'' as the tumblers fell into place. Suspense built up as he made the last turn of the knob. Grasping the lever, he flung the safe open, to the great amazement of young Harry, who later told his friends that his Uncle Fred could ''crack'' a safe. He never told Harry that he had remembered the combination all that time.

Dad was an inveterate inventor, always thinking up some idea to do things easier or better, but he obtained only one patent on his many supposedly good ideas, some of which had already been patented. He and Guadalupe Buelna from Santa Barbara obtained the original patents to the swinging arm sprinkler, which they manufactured at a small shop just below the railroad tracks in Santa Barbara. The idea was a good one and they undoubtedly would have made a fortune had they sold the royalties to their patent to some large manufacturer, but they tried to make and sell their product and were overwhelmed by the number of people who infringed on their patents. While they had the local market pretty well to themselves, they could not afford to contest all who stole their patents, as a large concern would have been able to do.

Our mother, Mercedes Dibblee Poett, was the daughter of Thomas Dibblee and Francisca de la Guerra. She was the sterner of our parents, as she had to put up with the day-to-day guidance of three young children who were just a little over a year apart in age. It was not until fourteen years later that another brother, Harold, was added to the fold. Mercedes was the only one among her five sisters and two brothers to choose to live on the ranch after the division of the property in 1918. Our mother had her heart set on drawing Los Yridises, which was on the northeasternmost reaches of San Julian and stretched from the valley floor all the way up to the top of the Santa Rosa Hills. From there one can see both San Julian and Santa Ynez Valley and view the magnificent mile-wide timber belt of canyon live oaks, which spreads three and a half miles in an easterly and westerly direction. The canyon follows the beds of Monterey shale that were delineated by the anticline-sincline structures of the region, and were originally beds of diatomaceous earth, some of which had been changed by a process of metamorphosis of heat and pressure to their present state of chert. At the western end of these geologic structures, the beds of diatomaceous earth more or less maintain their original state, so that the material can readily be mined by the open-pit process.

Mother had even chosen a site for a house on a mound at Yridises before the 1918 drawing took place. When she drew Los Yridises at the event, which was held at the Casa with all of the participants and their children, everyone was happy for her. A bottle of old Tapo brandy, made from the grapes at the Tapo ranch once owned by José de la Guerra, was opened to celebrate the drawing.

Mercedes Dibblee Poett (right) with friends Teresa Yndart (center) and Sally Stow, picking wildflowers on the ranch around 1900.

My father being of a more lenient disposition, it was up to Mother to make their children toe the line; not so hard when we were nearby, but when we were off on our own, she could not foresee and prohibit us from climbing the tallest Norfolk Island pine in Santa Barbara. The tree, from which we could overlook most of Santa Barbara, was right in our backyard. When she saw three of her children, aged six, seven, and eight, nearly at the top of the tall tree she nearly had a fit. It was with great trepidation that we climbed down its pitchy trunk.

Neither could she foresee that we would eat the poisonous berries of the castor plant and the scotch broom, both of which put us to sleep and meant that our stomachs had to be pumped out. Fortunately, our family doctor, Harold Sidebotham, was on call, and we made it through the ordeal—never to forage again on poisonous plants. Luckily, we never ate from the deadly oleander, which surely would have done us in.

On San Julian, we never sampled the plants, as we were most interested in the wild strawberries and blackberries that proliferate here. We seem to have been less troublesome at the ranch than in town; our energies were more often directed at climbing oak or sycamore trees, from which we never fell. The topography of the ranch usually took away a lot of our surplus energies.

This is not to imply that we did not suffer the usual bumps, scratches, and bruises of active kids, but most were minor. However, there was a time we were out under the arbor when a mare with colt was being used for some purpose. In a moment when no one was looking, I went over and pulled the mare's tail. The mare put her hind foot against me and threw me about fifteen feet. Had she kicked me hard, it is likely that I might have suffered a serious injury. Needless to say, after that I always kept my distance from a horse's hind feet.

Mother does not seem to have worried unduly about us when we were on horseback, as we turned out to be pretty good riders and did not take too many chances, realizing that we would be grounded if something serious happened to us. Our horses seem to enjoy us riding them as much as we did, for we were so light and they had been used to heavy loads.

On the ranch, mother taught us never to leave trash around or to harm any plants or animals that we found, although we were allowed to pick the exotically fragrant shooting star or wild cyclamen, which we found in the late winter or early spring. Mother was the first ecologist I ever knew, long before the word was ever heard. She would not allow pollution of the environment whatsoever.

Mother allowed the cutting of timber on Yridises only when shown that nearly all of the oaks cut would grow back from the old stump. Our oak forest is now very nearly as dense as it was sixty years ago when we first started cutting timber for firewood. Many of the trees that had been cut and had grown back are ready to be cut again, and since the new

Frederica and Harold Poett, 1921.

growth comes back in clusters, most of the new trees can be cut away, leaving the straightest to get all of the sunlight and nourishment from the root. Clear cutting is permitted only on ridge tops, where the forestry people recommend that this be done in order to allow for the construction of firebreaks.

Like many other Dibblees, Mercedes had a stubborn streak and would not let me raise anything but shorthorn cattle while she owned Yridises.

She deeded the property over to her children so as to minimize the threat of high inheritance taxes after her death. She outlived all of her brothers and sisters, four of whom were younger. She died at the ripe old age of ninety-one, having seen the coming of the train, the automobile, the airplane, and even men on the moon, which must have been a little

Frederica Dibblee Poett

hard for her to comprehend—being lucid until the very end, she accepted the moon landing with an open mind.

Mother was rigid in her code of conduct. As we grew up she did not mind us drinking or smoking (the last of which only Frederica did), but these must be done in moderation. None of us imbibed too freely or caroused unduly. Nothing should ever be done to sully the good names of Dibblee or Poett, she used to tell us. She was a stoic who had become crippled after an operation for an enlarged aorta; she lost her right leg and had to use a walker and crutches for the rest of her life. She never complained about the handicap, even though it caused her activities to be curtailed, especially her gardening, which she dearly loved to do. She smoked her Bull Durham cigarittos until the very end.

In the early part of the twentieth century, most of the Redingtons of San Francisco and Hillsborough came to Santa Barbara to live.

Arthur, the eldest son of Julia Poett and John Redington, and his wife Emily raised two daughters in Santa Barbara, but later moved back to

Harold Poett, 1946

Hillsborough. Arthur's sister Julia married Francis Wilson and lived on Pedregosa Street (next to the house that was occupied by John, Alfred, Lawrence, and Sarah Redington); this was on the west corner of Pedregosa and Santa Barbara streets. Theirs was a two-story wooden house constructed.

The Redingtons were good friends of our parents and sometimes asked us to Sunday breakfast. The Chinese cook would be instructed to make up a large serving of pancakes, which we avidly consumed with delicious maple syrup. Our host kept calling for more and more pancakes as we seemingly had insatiable appetites for the delicious rice pancakes. Finally, his batch of batter all gone, the cook would stick his head into the serving window and announce in a loud voice, "Pancake no more."

The lively conversation that bounced around the table from the sharp Irish wit of our elders usually left us agog with wonder at how such reparté could emerge so soon. Conundrums, limericks, and verse sprang to life on these occasions. Once as we were going in to breakfast and passing an open cloak closet, my dad playfully shoved Lawrence into the closet. He locked the door, saying, "You can't come out until you make a pun," at which Lawrence immediately replied, "Please opun the door."

Mary Stent and Margaret Kimball, together with William Howard of Sacramento and Marion Mitchell-Innis of Dumier, England, are the last Poett cousins of our generation still living, although there are many of the next generation alive at this writing.

Afred Redington started an insurance business on the north corner of State and Canon Perdido streets in Santa Barbara; his brother Jack had an office in the bank just across the street in the Commercial Bank. Lawrence married Josephine Parrott of San Francisco and left Santa Barbara to live in the Bay area. The Wilsons and the rest of the Redingtons lived out their lives in Santa Barbara.

During World War I, when the influenza epidemic of 1917–18 was at its worst, most of the Dibblees and the Poetts came to the ranch thinking that if we got away from the city there would be less chance of contracting the malady. But when one of our tenants died on the ranch, we decided that it might be better to go back to town, where there could be care from a doctor.

The winter of 1917–18 was a particularly bad one for the ranchers, as the rains held off until nearly the end of February. The cattle got thin and many of them died of starvation, since it was not possible to obtain any alfalfa hay when we needed it, and the only feed we could get was timothy, which was all right for horses but does not have enough protein for cattle.

When the rains finally came, the storms lasted interminably, and caused bogs into which the cattle would get stuck and have to be pulled out by a *vaquero* on horseback. He would throw his reata over the cow's head or horns and drag it from the mire. Then the rider would dismount his horse to take the rope off the animal's head and she would often stagger to her feet and take out after the rider, collapsing after a few steps. These animals had to have hay brought to them or they would die; only about half of those pulled from the bogs lived.

Our losses that year were staggering; upwards of three hundred cows died that winter. One old cow was brought back to headquarters on a sled. We dug holes in the ground for her legs to extend into so that she wouldn't lie down; she was given a bottle of precious brandy, but died anyway.

Mud was everywhere and transportation was difficult; chains had to be used most of the time on the car's wheels, as the roads were all dirt (or rather, mud). We went back to town in November 1918, when the epidemic was at its peak. I caught the bug and was confined to bed for about three weeks. Since then, I have never been inoculated for any of the flu bugs that go around, and have never caught any of them.

After that disastrous year, silos were constructed on San Julian, as well as on the neighboring Hollister ranches, in an effort to stave off such disasters. The silos were filled with chopped corn raised on the farming fields. Oat hay was raised and stored loose in barns and in stacks outside and covered with tarpaulins. Not one year has passed since then that we have not had a fairly large reserve of hay to get us through a bad winter.

After a few years of stacking loose hay, the ranch obtained a horse-powered baler—powered by horses going around in a circle, pulling a rod attached to a worm-gear. It was a slow process, but the air-cooled engine soon superceded the horses; later the pick-up baler came into use.

For some years, we raised alfalfa hay on the ranch and irrigated some of our fields adjacent to the creek, where we had certain prescriptive rights to take and store water. Power rates have risen too high to warrant the cost of pumping versus the cost of alfalfa purchased from such areas as the San Joaquin or Imperial valleys. One year some neighbors purchased a thousand tons of alfalfa hay from the Imperial Valley and fed a large bunch of cattle on that hay. But their pasture field was not large enough to keep the cattle scattered; the concentration of cattle feces spread stomach and lung worms among them, and many made little or no growth gains. Now the smart cattleman buys good, leafy alfalfa hay, which can be stored for several years, and often staves off disaster in a poor year.

After several years, the silos were abandoned and all of them have fallen or been taken down; pit silos are more efficient. Most ranchers hate to feed silage, a chore relegated to dairymen, despite many advantages of ensilage.

When I was running cattle on Yridises, from the 1930's to the 1950's, the University of California extension service was pushing the use of a high-protein supplement with added salt to limit the intake of the meal. I had started using molasses to supplement our cattle. The feed had to be taken out to the cattle each day because if it was fed to them in troughs, they would eat too much of the sweet stuff and get "scours." It was not until about the early 1950's that a company in San Luis Obispo came out with a bitter substance made from beet pulp that would limit the intake of the molasses. It could be delivered directly by truck into our feed troughs scattered about the ranch.

The university extension service would never admit the advantage of using carbohydrates over high-protein feed until late in the 1960's, when the molasses with the bitter additive was made available.

During the time I was buying molasses in bulk, a little boy—the son of a ranch hand—opened the valve of the tank of molasses shortly after the five thousand-gallon tank had been filled. When I came home that evening I saw that molasses had flowed across the farmyard and down the creek a hundred yards away. The entire load had been lost onto the ground.

In the early part of the century, when I first came to San Julian, the ranch was self-sufficient and produced most of the food that was consumed by the large crew of men there. There was a slaughterhouse where beef, mutton, and pork were prepared. Pork was often smoked for ham and bacon, and the lard was rendered in a large cast-iron pot. Cracklings were a result of the lard-rendering process. The beef was nearly always cow meat and not as tender or fat as our modern-day beef.

We had our own flock of sheep that were tended by our last shepherd, a Basque named Gaston Sorrhondo, who became a member of the fence crew when the sheep were sold in the late twenties. In earlier times, many more sheep were slaughtered, as Uncle Henry Dibblee preferred mutton to beef; it was said that he had mutton nearly every day. We would corn (in salt brine) or jerk (dry) a considerable amount of beef as we did not have any refrigeration. When the gas line came through in the mid-twenties, a liquid-ammonia compressor was installed and a walk-in box constructed. Then the meat would keep for two weeks or so.

There was a small herd of milk cows, tended by the chore-man. He often took care of the vegetable garden and fed the chickens, gathered the eggs, and fed the hogs from barley we raised. We raised our own potatoes in the loamy sand of a nearby field (potatoes were stored in barrels of sawdust), as well as onions and garlic.

The large vegetable garden produced corn, tomatoes, chiles, squash, cucumbers, lettuce, celery, beets, musk- and watermelon, Hubbard and other squashes, and pumpkins. In winter we grew cabbage, cauliflower, Brussel sprouts, turnips, beets, and herbs.

The orchard down by the county road supplied us with cherries, plums, apples, apricots, peaches, pears, quince, and figs. The quince and apples were made into preserves, as was a yellow Portuguese pumpkin we called *barbarie*. Apples, apricots, figs, and prunes were dried in a large cabinet-like structure that contained many screened shelves to contain the drying fruit. All of this demanded quite a lot of labor, but it was cheap in those days and worth the trouble.

All that was needed to be purchased was sugar, flour, coffee, tea, salt, baking powder, and spices. Many of the groceries were shipped down by steamer (before my time) from the San Francisco firm of wholesale grocers, Wellman & Peck. We roasted and ground our own coffee, sometimes sent to us in sacks from Southern America.

When the automobile became popular and the crew of men was diminished by the use of the large Caterpillar tractor, groceries became more readily available and we made trips to Lompoc more and more frequently. We bought most groceries in the early days from F.I. Callis in Lompoc. The stage line had ceased to function when the railroad went by to Santa Barbara, so we had to go into Lompoc for our mail about once or twice a week.

A Western Union telephone line ran through the ranch to Lompoc. So many neighbors had hooked into the line, which by that time had become our private property, we had to force them off the line; there was far too much palaver and many times we could not get through. However, one of these neighbors, through whose property the line ran, resented this. When our line went out in a 1941 storm, he would not let us onto his land to repair it. It was another ten years without telephone communication before we installed a radio telephone.

We had moved to Los Yridises in 1919, having constructed a house on a mound where my mother had decided she would like to live. The house we built consisted almost entirely of redwood lumber that had been saved from the two-story Poett house at 325 East Mission Street in Santa Barbara. It had been torn down and rebuilt on the ranch as a single-story house. When we came to live at San Julian, my sister Nan and I rode five miles to school near the ranch house, or we drove in a sulky cart drawn by a fine white horse that had been given to us by a James Cornwall, a contractor in Santa Barbara and a friend of my father. The horse's name was Doc and he would trot along the road at a fast pace, often racing our neighbors' children, whose buggy was not as flexible as our sulky. Rain or shine, we got to school on time, and were always home before dark. We hardly ever caught colds because we were made to change our clothes if they were wet. This went on for three years until we graduated, and moved back to Santa Barbara.

Poett House in Santa Barbara

The ranch, however, was always on our minds. Living on land such as ours, one forms an attachment to the land when times are happy, when we had our animals and enjoyed the freedom of the ranch. I moved back to the ranch in 1934, and have been living here ever since.

Nan and I, more than any others of our generation, formed a strong love for the land. We knew where the sweet-smelling shooting stars grew, when to expect the wild violets, where to look for the exotic Mariposa lilies. We delighted in showing visiting botanists where the trilliums, false Solomon seal, and other exotic plants grew, although we never divulged the location of the Woodwardia ferns.

I think I know how the Indians felt about the land and how they loved everything in nature. And love of the land means a respect for it—it means that you do not destroy anything unnecessarily, nor create conditions whereby the elements can destroy, such as by overgrazing or burning off timber and brush to create more pasture. It means living with Nature and accepting her ways, however drastic it may seem.

In my early days on the ranch, there were many workers, most of whom were teamsters; there were six teams of six horses to do the plowing and tilling the land. This did not last many years, because the horses ate up too much hay.

Besides the teamsters, there was Jasper Biraholm, the blacksmith, a stableman, a choreman, three or four *vaqueros*, a foreman, a cook, and a harnessmaker, who was kept busy making and mending harnesses for nearly two dozen horses and mending bridles and saddles for the riders. The leather harnesses were always black—why I do not know. The blacksmith was kept busy shoeing horses and keeping the plow shears sharp.

In the spring, Jasper was needed to poison squirrels; there was no countrywide policy for controlling the pests. He would mix barley with molasses and strychnine. As he added the strychnine he would taste the batch to see if it was bitter enough. He never seemed to suffer any ill effects and perhaps had built up an immunity to small doses of the poison, as some of the kings of ancient times did. The least little bit of cyanide would have finished him, though. He could tolerate arsenic as well.

The family celebrates a birthday at the ranch in 1918. Standing (from left) are Francisca "Quica" de la Guerra Dibblee, William T. Summers, William Dibblee, and Frank Underhill. Seated are Nan Poett, Alfred R. Poett, and Mercedes Dibblee Poett.

Our Grandmother Quica, a good Catholic, always ate fish on Fridays. Many times she had to call Dr. Sidebotham on Saturdays to come when she became ill. He deduced that she had eaten some shellfish, and those are known to contain a fairly high concentration of arsenic, to which she was not tolerant.

Dr. Harold Sidebotham was a tall, jolly Englishman. Our family doctor, he was the epitome of the absent-minded professor. Sidebotham in the early days drove about Santa Barbara in a buggy. Once when he visited a patient, he carried his little black satchel into the house. While he was there, one of the other occupants of the house had called for the hairdresser, who also came in a buggy and tied her horse at the same

T. Wilson Dibblee and Ynez Dibblee at El Paseo
during the first Old Spanish Days Fiesta in 1924.

tying rack as had the doctor. The hairdresser stopped on her way out of the house, set her satchel near the door, and went to converse with someone. Dr. Sidie, as we fondly called him, saw the lady's satchel on his way out and picked it up, thinking it was his own. He left the house and took off in the hairdresser's buggy. He realized his mistake when he called on his next patient and opened the satchel to get his stethoscope. To his amazement, and chagrin, he found curling irons, scissors, and the hairdresser's other paraphernalia.

Dr. Sidie used to regale us with stories of his experiences as a surgeon in the British Army. Some of his most successful surgeries occurred on the battlefields in India, where there were few antiseptics except fresh air and sunlight. He was very much interested in astronomy and was acquainted with George Ellery Hale of the California Institute of Technology. When a total eclipse of the sun occurred in 1926, many of the scientists along the coast of Southern California came to San Julian because of the chance of heavy fog lying along the lowlands near the shore. We all went up to one of our high hills, where we were able to view the eclipse. As totality approached, the chickens went in to roost, and the coyotes bayed their mournful howls, echoing eerily over the hills.

Wilson Dibblee

Wilson Dibblee was a tall, handsome man with a gentle manner, and I never knew him to raise his voice or use unacceptable language. He was El Patrón to all of the men, and they were always respectful to the gentleman. Wilson was considered "the last of the Dons" by many. He rode his fine palomino or chestnut stallion down State Street at Santa Barbara's annual fiesta. Pleasant to converse with, with a well-modulated voice and perfect diction, Wilson had been educated at Thacher School in Ojai, to which he would ride at the beginning of the semester. He went on to the University of California at Berkeley, where he graduated with a degree in law. After college, he became a banker, and, together with his brother-in-law, William T. Summers, was successful in establishing and selling banks throughout California. They would start a bank and, once it was well established, sell it to a larger or more well-known bank.

Wilson Dibblee and William Summers first started a bank in San Luis Obispo, then San Francisco, Santa Barbara, and other places. Summers had been in the banking business before he joined with Wilson. He took his bride, Panchita Dibblee, to Nome in the Alaska Territory, then

Costumed family members gathered on the veranda of Casa de la Guerra during the first Old Spanish Days Fiesta in 1924. Standing (from left) are Mercedes Dibblee Poett, T. Wilson Dibblee, Ynez Dibblee, and A. Dibblee Poett. Seated are Carmen Dibblee Underhill, Herminia de la Guerra Lee, Francisca de la Guerra Dibblee, Delfina de la Guerra, and Harold Poett.

Hawaii, and back to San Francisco, where they started the Merchants National Bank. Altogether, I think Panchita and Billy Summers must have lived in a least a dozen cities and towns during his banking career.

Wilson Dibblee's last bank was the Central Bank in Santa Barbara. He sold it to Bank of America just before the 1925 earthquake, which did quite a bit of damage to the tall structure. Wilson then moved into El Paseo, where he successfully managed the properties of Bernhard Hoffmann, who had bought the old de la Guerra adobe and constructed El Paseo de la Guerra in downtown Santa Barbara.

At the same time, Wilson ran the ranch as general manager. He loved to stay at the ranch; the family lived in Santa Barbara.

In the early 1940's, Wilson, looking for a herd bull to replace the bull Cluny Royal Windsor that had died, decided to drive to Canada; he invited me and took along his son, Richard, and the herdsman, Gallagher, to see what he could get. In his big, comfortable Packard sedan we "ate up the miles" through California, Nevada, and Idaho as we headed for Saskatchewan, where we had heard of a good herd of shorthorn cattle.

Visiting farms along the way to look over the cattle, I found I was able to recall most of the bulls when I placed their position relative to others or the barn, silo, or other structure. When we arrived outside Calgary, we started looking at some cattle. Wilson got too close to a cow with a calf and was bowled over and broke his glasses. A couple of days of recuperation, and he was all right again.

After finding a bull, we headed for the Athabaska Glacier, but were unable to reach it; the roads were too slippery from a recent oiling. We headed for Banff, taking the waters of the region. And then home down the coasts of Washington, Oregon, and northern California.

The bull we had picked out arrived at Gaviota a few weeks later and was brought to the ranch. About a year after he arrived, he began to ail and then died. A postmortem by our vet revealed that a nail the bull had swallowed had punctured its liver. The insurance company paid us the value of the bull, but that was the last of the purebred shorthorn bulls ever bought to head up the herd. It had consumed too much time and money over nearly twenty-five years.

When I was growing up on the ranch, Wilson Dibblee used to ask me, "How is the grass in the Pacífico?" or "What is the condition of the cattle in El Jaro?" I learned to observe those things, which stood me in such good stead in later years when I took over the management of Yridises and later, after Wilson's death in 1952, of San Julian.

Bill Dibblee

Wilson's young brother, Bill Dibblee, also attended the University of California at Berkeley, but never pursued any particular career. Instead, he dabbled in mining stocks, owning interests in mines in San Luis Obispo County, a gold mine near Castaic, and various interests in Mexico. He was a tall, handsome fellow who loved to roam around San

Julian at night. Having once had a job at the Edison plant in Santa Barbara, he had learned to stay up late during the dark of night and sleep much of the morning. Bill loved to stay up all night, playing poker or dining out with his many lady friends. He was nearly always in financial straits and had to be bailed out by Wilson, who did not want him to lose his ranch, Los Palos Colorados. Diatomaceous earth was later discovered on Bill's property, and the income enabled him to live as he had always desired—not lavishly, but comfortably.

Bill Dibblee was a great collector of antique automobiles and had a Stutz Bearcat, a Willys-Overland, and an old Packard, among his other cars. Bill would buy and store away unused batteries, coils of underground cable on huge spools, and all manner of surplus junk, much of it useless. He had a merry twinkle in his eye and his face would light up as he listened to or recounted a good story. His late morning sleeps, however, were a headache, as I often found it difficult to find the time to confer with him about ranch affairs.

The Dibblee Daughters

On the distaff side, Panchita was the eldest of the seven surviving children of Thomas and Francisca Dibblee; their eldest daughter, Teresa, had died of tuberculosis at the age of twenty. Panchita, also called Pep, was the liveliest of the lot, always thinking of amusing things to do or say. She would never take a siesta, fearing that something might happen during her inactivity and she would miss it. She was a dynamo. Like Delfina, Panchita did not like to cook.

Ynez, the next eldest, was the most talented; extremely graceful as well as beautiful, she would most likely have attained great prominence in her career as a dancer. During a long stay in Spain as a young lady, she learned first-hand from the gypsies of Granada how to dance the real flamenco. A stage career was not considered "correct" for young ladies of the day, and her great talents were never allowed to reach full bloom. She wrote some creditable poetry, which she published, and many plays, which were unpublished.

Ynez, Delfina, and Carmen, all of whom had been schooled abroad,

Ynez Dibblee was a beautiful and talented dancer.

spoke impeccable French. When they conversed in that language, which we did not understand as children, we decided to invent our own, a ''B'' language, which we could rattle off without the adults understanding us. We even went so far as to mix it with Spanish, which none of our friends could fathom.

Our mother, Mercedes, was next in line. She was born in 1879, two years to the day later than my father. Fred Poett and Mercedes Dibblee were married on their birthdays.

When I was about two years old in 1909, we moved to a farm near Arroyo Grande. Why we moved I never knew, but we had a governess

James Poett (left), William de la
Guerra Poett and Susan Dibblee Poett
(above), children of Harold Poett.

named Millie. Millie was a little simple, and my father used to tease her
by saying, "I am your Uncle Dudley."

"You ain't my Uncle Dudley," Millie replied.

"How do you know?"

"I've never seen you before."

"Have you ever seen a hippopotamus before?"

"No."

"Well, then, I am your Uncle Dudley."

And Millie would be completely baffled by this "logic."

We did not stay long in Arroyo Grande, however, and returned to Santa
Barbara to live at our grandfather's house on East Mission Street. It was
there that I well remember being carried to the porch one night in 1910
to see Halley's comet, which was huge, with its long tail sweeping
nearly a quarter way across the sky.

Mother's next sister, the next in line after Wilson, was Carmelita, who
was vivacious and full of fun and played the piano with great verve.

Joseph Russell, Caroline Russell, and Delfina Russell Mott, children of "Nan" Mercedes and C.E. Russell.

Walker Tompkins told a tale (for which I cannot vouch) about how Carmelita once was at a ball, where she happened to be overheard saying she would love to go abroad and see Egypt and the Holy Land. Later in the evening, so the tale goes, she was introduced to a handsome gentleman whose name was Francis Underhill.

She said to him, "And who are you, Mr. Underhill?"

To which he supposedly replied, "I am the man who is going to take you to Egypt on my yacht"—which he did after they were married.

They were a handsome couple, and she adored her Frankie. Underhill had defended the Americas Cup two times, and was a man "easily satisfied with the best." Carmelita was struck with polio and became lame, but she outlived Frank Underhill by nearly forty years.

Bill Dibblee was the next to the last of the children of Thomas and Francisca. Delfina, called "Doña Babe" by the servants, was the last.

My father and Bill Dibblee jointly became involved in the day-to-day operations of the ranch in the late twenties, after the services of John Troup had been dispensed with, but before the unfortunate racehorse business had been established. They acted as foreman and superintendent, keeping the ranch books and overseeing the twelve or fifteen men comprising the work crew.

Anita Oreña Dibblee and her grandchildren (from left): Clasen Hoyt, Mrs. Dibblee, Richard Donohoe, Joseph Donohoe, Anita Dibblee, Wilson Dibblee Donohoe; seated on Mrs. Dibblee's lap: Dibblee and Antonia Hoyt.

At that time, there was a fence crew operating full-time, fencing off the various parcels of land in anticipation of some of the new owners taking over their own properties. Wilson Dibblee was still general manager of the large Dibblee Heirs operation, but there were some owners of various parcels who were dissatisfied with the operations; when a racehorse operation was started in the mid-thirties, four of the seven decided to pull out and run cattle on their own pieces or lease them out.

The racehorse operation necessitated the services of a jockey, a trainer, and a stable man, who was occupied nearly full-time in keeping the stables clean and the horses groomed. A government remount stud was secured and a racetrack constructed. The horses were sent to the races—mostly claiming races—and the operation was maintained at considerable cost and without the prospects for any substantial gains. After ten years of heavy losses, the venture was abandoned.

<h1 style="text-align:center">III.</h1>

THE FENCE CREW enclosed the various parcels that had not been separated from one another. The fence line on Yridises was built between it and Las Ytias of Francisca "Panchita" Summers, and the boundary line between Yridises and Los Llanitos, which had not been fenced on the line, was altered. A fence between Las Ytias and Los Palos Colorados was built, and other boundary fences between San Julian and our neighbors repaired.

There had been a subdivision survey of San Julian made in 1918 by Frank Flournoy, a surveyor who used the earlier Poett survey as a general guide; the survey was slightly refined and new boundary markers were put in place. However, in the interim between then and the actual fencing, nearly twenty years had elapsed and many of the boundary markers had been dislodged, burned over, or simply rotted out. My dad revived his father's old theodolite, and we had to relocate the missing stakes or markers. That is how I came to be familiar with the use of a fine Zeiss instrument. When the second war started and the Army Corps of Engineers at Camp Cook (now Vandenberg Air Force Base) put out an urgent appeal for surveying instruments, I sold the old instrument thinking that someday I might get it back. I have lived to regret the action.

My dad and I, together with a brush crew from the ranch, were able to redefine Flournoy's survey. The new fences followed precisely on the boundary markers. In one case, however, there was a dispute with a neighbor who thought that the boundary line between his land and that of Bill Dibblee went up the old abandoned county road, when actually it zigzagged down by the main creek. He fenced off the land using the old road, and when Bill saw the fence there he was furious and ordered the ranch crew to tear it out; they did so, to the chagrin of the neighbor. After that, there was bad blood between the two that lasted until Bill's death. The neighbor was clearly in the wrong and should have apologized.

Most fence posts in the old days were put into place in holes dug by hand; it would take two men from fifteen to thirty minutes of hard work to dig a hole and tamp the post in place. To do this, the corner posts were first put into place, and a strand of barbed wire strung between them so that a straight line could be established; generally five strands of wire were used. As soon as the digging crew had the posts in place, they were followed by two men stringing the wire. It was hard work, but the men kept at the job, headed by Juan "Banca" Laranetta, a large Basque with only one good eye. When steel posts became available, about ten or fifteen of those would be driven into the ground with a hand tamper, and then a wooden post would be placed to keep the fence straight (too long a stretch of iron posts can be made to lean). The fence wire in the timber—if protected from the fog, which carries a certain amount of salt—will last longer than that on the exposed ridges or those close to the ocean. Some of the old galvanized ribbon wire placed along the boundary lines is still in good condition after one hundred years, the zinc galvanizing having been put on much heavier in the old days.

In some areas where the brush is heavy, the fences stand a long time unless the brush is burned, and then the posts fall and the wires rust out right away. We find it best not to burn along the fence lines so as not to disturb the zinc. Much of the barbed wire now sold on the American market comes from Korea, and the coils of wire, stacked on freighter decks, bear witness to the salt that has accumulated during the sea voyage. It is well to wash this salt off before using the wire. Now, wire and posts are priced about ten times higher than they were in the '30s; iron posts are commensurately priced. Redwood posts are scarce, if available at all. There is no substitute for a redwood post, many of which have lasted us fifty or even a hundred years. Cattle raising as we know it would be impractical if not impossible without modern fencing, something W.W. Hollister realized nearly a century ago, to his great credit.

Once in a while a rancher or farmer will raise an animal that has no respect for fences and can slip through most any barbed wire, but when calves are brought up to respect an electric fence installed in a sudan or alfalfa field, they hardly ever bother a good barbed wire fence.

We have many miles of fence along the state highway that bisects our ranch, much of which was installed prior to 1964, when the Highway Department started putting the fence on the state side of the line. The result is that we are obliged to maintain the fence that is on our property. Automobiles often crash through the fences, and if our animals stray onto the highway as a result of such an incident and someone is hurt or killed, we might be held liable for the damages, with the result that our liability insurance rates are extremely high. Where the fence line is on state land, the burden for maintaining the fence and the liability is incurred by the state, but even so, if someone is injured or killed by our cattle or those of our tenants, we could be involved in lawsuits that might last many years.

After the death of William Dibblee, which followed that of his brother Wilson by about fourteen years, it became evident that San Julian would be lost to the Dibblees if something was not done to alleviate the tax situation, whereby much land would have to be sold in order to pay the heavy federal and state inheritance taxes. After much consultation, it was deemed advisable for the aunts to form a trust and to turn over their interest in the home piece, consisting of some 4,000 acres and the Casa San Julian, to the second generation to hold in trust for the third generation, who would receive it tax free. Fairly heavy gift taxes were assessed on the donors, but they were able to stand the cost, and now that action ensures that our nieces, nephews, and cousins will some day have the land. It will then be up to them to arrange transfers to their children or cousins if the land is to stay in the family.

Fires

In the early days in California, there was no organized way to fight fires. One disastrous fire in 1857 cost the de la Guerras dearly. The following year was a drought year, and many cattle, which might otherwise have been saved by San Julian had the ranch not been burned over, died on Simi.

When the railroad came through the Hollister Ranch in 1903, it became the practice of the train crews to clear the flues of the locomotives by throwing sand into the fire, which would then sweep the chimneys of soot. But the sparks thus generated often started fires along the right-of-way, fires that often spread to the Hollisters' adjacent pastures. One such fire in 1925 burned north all the way over the hills of the Hollister Ranch and stopped only when it came to the large barranca on San Julian.

Soon after that, a lightning fire started on Yridises, but it was not of long duration and did not do much damage. Many fires were caused by the Las Ytias charcoal burners, who persisted in burning the brush and tree trimmings. I remember once having to leave the radio, which was reporting the sinking of the *Graf Spee* in Montevideo harbor during the early part of the war, to put out a Las Ytias fire.

Occasional fires that were supposed to be control burns got away from the fire crews, but material damage was seldom done to the pastures. Only the fences suffered. The large oak forest on Yridises, which, according to Vicente Guevarra, was badly damaged in a fire in 1901, has not seen any large amount of damage except for a fire of unknown origin that swept onto Los Yridises and El Álamo, to the west, in 1976. This fire was driven onto our land by a strong wind one hot summer day, and nearly burned down our barn and farmhouse. We had good water pressure and the state, county, federal, and Vandenberg fire departments were all here with about ten pumper trucks, five or six bulldozers, and about a hundred men, who managed to contain the blaze. Airplanes were also used to drop fire retardant chemicals on the fire, which was extremely difficult to fight on account of the heavy oak forest. The job was well coordinated by having one man who knew his business run the whole operation. Considerable damage was done to a fence line that, fortunately, was insured against fire. Many oak trees died as a result of the hot blaze, which is unusual, as oak trees will generally survive a fire. Many of those trees that died were cut and the timber was sold the following year. Since that time, we have instituted a program of cutting wide swaths on some of the ridges, which should allow future fires to be contained a little more easily.

The six silos on San Julian, built in 1918-19, were constructed on top of large circular concrete bases, and the fermented corn juice used to trickle down and accumulate there. The men could go to the silos and collect the fermented liquor, which could easily be distilled to make a potent whiskey, but not very many of them became inebriated.

In 1918 our uncle, Harry Poett, who owned the two-story house on Mission Street in Santa Barbara, decided to have the structure torn down and replaced with a smaller house. A wrecker named Doan was engaged to dismantle the structure (consisting almost entirely of redwood except for the floor joists and rafters). The lumber was saved and hauled to Yridises, where my mother had previously decided to have it rebuilt, but in a different configuration. An architect was hired, and the new one-story house was built on a mound about a mile and a half from the state highway running through San Julian. During the summer the house was being built, we camped up the canyon beside a flowing stream; the following winter, we moved into the house, shortly after my younger brother Harold was born.

Our grandmother, Francisca "Quica" Dibblee, generally came to the ranch in the middle of summer with her two unmarried daughters, Ynez and Delfina. They would come laden with enough trunks, boxes, and suitcases for an extended stay abroad. Many of the boxes and bags were never opened and became the brunt of numerous jokes about all that superfluous luggage. Juan "Toto," the family's Cuban-Chinese cook, and Elvira Corpas, a Spanish maid, were brought along.

Elvira used to correct our Spanish pronunciation, trying to make us lisp as the Castellaños do, but we scorned her teaching as unsuitable for Californians. Between our grandmother and her daughters and Toto and Elvira we became fluent in Spanish, but like most foreign languages, it

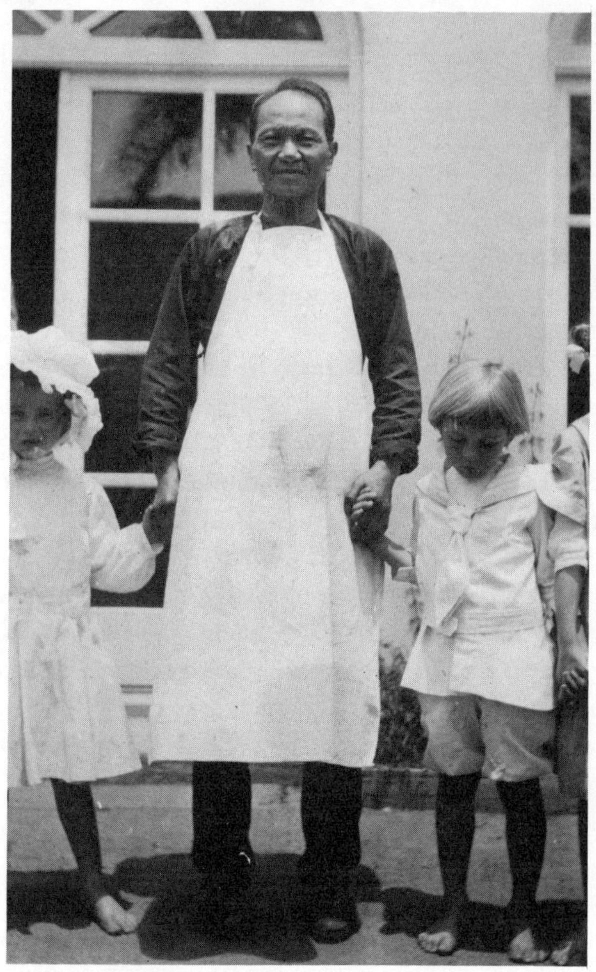

Juan Toto with Nan and Dibblee Poett about 1910.

was mostly forgotten by many of my cousins and brother and sisters. I, however, took Spanish grammar in high school and have had the opportunity of speaking the language almost continually with workers on the ranch, have kept up with my Spanish, so that I can converse readily except in political and technical terms. Many of the men working on the ranch in the old days were native Californians who spoke Spanish, and we had innumerable Spanish and Mexican sheepherders and tenants with whom

I spoke. But I was never able to converse with the many Portuguese who lived hereabouts, as their dialect was nearly always that of the Azores, and quite different speech from that of the mainland Portuguese.

Our grandmother Quica was beloved by all who knew her, and her every wish was our command—except for Alfredo, the choreman and handyman, who would argue with anyone. She was a tall, handsome woman of about fifty when I first knew her; she was nearly twenty-four years younger than her husband, Thomas Dibblee, whom she outlived by thirty-seven years. She died in 1932 at the age of nearly seventy-five. Our mother, Mercedes, outlived all the rest of her siblings and died at the age of ninety-one.

While we were living here at Yridises, friends would often drop in unexpectedly, since we had no telephone or mail delivery.

Dick Bond once came and asked if he could borrow a horse to ride over the hills to the Hollister Ranch. We had available that day only one horse, Cahuilla (which in Spanish referred to a two-bit piece; there was an expression current, *"Que no vale niuna cahuilla,"* meaning that something was not worth a cahuilla—not that the horse, a gift from Wilson and a favorite of Jim Rios, was describable as such, but it had reached the age of a pensioner).

Cahuilla had been raised at Casa San Julian, so when Dick rode the horse over to the Hollister Ranch for a party, which lasted past midnight, he was told to let Cahuilla bring him home. The night was pitch dark, but the horse knew the trail and would stop at each wire gate, whereupon the rider would dismount, grope around for the gate, let the horse through, and mount to resume the eerie journey up and down the steep hills of Santa Anita and down the equally steep hillsides of San Julian. After about five or six of the gate openings, Cahuilla stopped in front of a barn that looked different from the one that Dick had left at Yridises, so he lit a match and discovered that the old horse had taken him back to his old stomping grounds, near the Casa San Julian. Dick arrived at Yridises about an hour later.

Marshall Bond, Dick's brother and one of my best friends, was called up by the draft and spent his war service in New Zealand. After his return, he became a writer and wrote books about his father's adventures in the Klondike.

Marshall Bond, their father, was a stockbroker in Santa Barbara and worked for Logan and Bryan on State and Carrillo streets. He never lost the gold fever and would go out to the desert every year seeking the precious metal. He was never successful in his quest, although he always believed that he came close to finding some of the legendary lost mines of the Mojave. This went on for at least twenty years, until Marshall senior's death.

We had some friends in Santa Barbara named Tallant who lived adjacent to us on Garden Street; they had one of the Crocker houses. We lived just around the corner on Mission. My dad and George Tallant were good friends and spent a lot of time together. George and Lita had two children, George and Genevieve, whom we called Gingy.

George Tallant had perfect pitch and a wonderful memory. Occasionally they would hear the bell of a locomotive pulling into the station near State Street.

Invariably George Tallant would say to my father, "Fred, do you hear that bell? That is old 7718 [or some other number he knew] of the Southern Pacific Railroad. The last time I heard that bell was—"

My dad would say, "Oh, George, you're crazy, you don't know what you're talking about."

"Well, how much will you bet?"

"Okay, let's check."

And they would go to the station, where George always won the bet. My dad could never figure out how George Tallent could tell and remember such a thing.

The Tallants were also friends of the Coopers, who lived over the hill from San Julian, about five miles as the owl flies. One late evening, while we were playing poker, we heard an owl hoot. George Tallant stopped the play and said, "Do you hear that owl?" We all said yes, to which he asserted that it was the same owl he had heard at Bill Cooper's the previous night. And none of us could say him nay.

Appendix

The Last Will of Juan Gutierre Guerra

IN DEI NOMINE. AMEN. Let all who see this letter and will know that I, Gutierre Guerra, legitimate son of Gutierre Pérez Guerra, lord of the castle-tower and ancestral grounds[1] of Ibio and doña[2] María Gómez de Belasco, his wife, who was the son of Count don[3] Pedro Guerra and doña María de Estrada, his wife, and grandson of Count don Pedro Guerra and doña Sancha González de Aguero, being that I am soon leaving to serve our majesty and King, wanting to leave my ancestral grounds with someone who will take care of them and who will protect and shelter his relatives, complying with the laws of Spain, respecting the nobility of said grounds and seeing that doña María Gómez de Belasco, my mother and lady,[4] and doña Inés de la Vega, my legitimate wife, are no longer living, having present Juan Gutiérrez Guerra, my oldest son who will maintain said ancestral grounds and who will protect and shelter his relatives, I name him to govern in my name said ancestral grounds, his brothers and relatives, and after my days he will be the lord of it, and will possess by ownership of said ancestral grounds, in addition, a third and a fifth[5] or the most that the castle-tower and ancestral grounds of Ibio with all its chattels can and should be worth, namely: wheels as well as ironworkings and windmills and waters, pastures, arable land and trees, woodland, public grazing pastures and livestock, along with the church of San Pedro and San Felices[6] and two-thirds of the tithes, as it appertains to me and to the said ancestral grounds of Ibio, and as it was possessed by my father, grandfather, and great-grandfather, Gonzalo Guerra and his wife Rosanda, my great-great grandparents, and Gonzalo Gómez and his wife Emilia Pérez, his parents, and Count Gonzalo and his wife Urraca, their grandparents and all my ancestors descended by legitimate line of male descendants from Count Sancho de Nava, brother of Count Rodrigo, sons of Prince Aldelgasten, son of King don Silo.

All of which and everything else that I have had and will have in Asturias de Santillana that belongs to the said ancestral grounds of Ibio, I leave for after my days to the said Juan Gutiérrez Guerra, my son, by right of primogeniture; and after his days, to Gonzalo Guerra, his oldest son, my grandson, and to all those that will succeed him and that are males capable of carrying on the lineage; in such manner that if the said Gonzalo Guerra, my grandson, were to die without leaving a male heir, the said property and ancestral grounds will belong to the other first legitimate son to be born to the said Juan Gutiérrez, my son. And if he were to die without leaving a male heir, said property and ancestral grounds will belong to the other first son to be born. And it shall proceed in this manner, degree by degree, whereupon if all the above-mentioned were to die without leaving a male heir, the said property and ancestral grounds will belong to the closest relative to the said grounds of Ibio and said Juan Gutiérrez, my son.

And to definitively state the authenticity of what is contained in this letter and everything pertaining to it, I waive all and any laws and rights that can or could act to the contrary and all other laws which in any way can act to the contrary to what is contained in this letter and will or in any part of it. And furthermore, I obligate myself, with all my property, furniture, real estate that I have and will have, to never say or do or otherwise act contrary to anything contained in this letter and will nor in any part of it, before having it done always rightly and justly, and if it were to be otherwise, it will not be valid. And for this document to be valid and not dubious, I declared said letter and will in the manner it is, in the presence of Pedro García de la Iseca, scribe of our majesty and King and notary public of his court and of all his kingdoms, whom I asked to write this letter and will, and to put his seal on it and to give it to the said Juan Gutiérrez, my son. It was made and declared on the ancestral grounds of Ibio, the third day of the month of February the year of the birth of our Lord Jesus Christ of one thousand three hundred and ninety-eight, with witnesses who were present to authenticate this, Pedro Vélez, resident of Villanueza, Juan González, resident of Ibio, and Sancho de Cieza, resident of Ferrera, and Cristóbal Ruiz, resident of Sierra.

The maker of the deed, whom I, the scribe, truly know, signed it with his name, Juan Gutierre Guerra; and I, said Juan García de la Iseca, scribe and notary public, above-mentioned, witness to the authenticity of this, was present among the said witnesses to the execution of the document such as it is. In testimony of truth, Juan Garcia de la Iseca.

NOTES:

1. *castle-tower* and *ancestral grounds*: "torre palacio" in the text refers to a castle with a tower, not just to the castle's tower; "solar" in the original means the nobility's ancestral estate lands, and includes the main dwelling, presumably the castle-tower, as well as the real estate belonging to the noble family.

2. *doña*: This, as well as the masculine "don," was left in the original Spanish because it was felt too presumptuous to assign these titles English equivalents such as Sir and Lady, because they actually are not equivalents at all, only approximations. Don and Doña are Spanish titles given to gentlemen and ladies of noble lineage.

3. *don*: (see 2 above)

4. *lady*: This approximation of the Spanish *señora* denotes the most respected matriarchal figure associated with a noble family.

5. *a third and a fifth* means exactly that—one-third plus one-fifth, which equals in common terms eight-fifteenths (five fifteenths—or one-third—plus three fifteenths—or one fifth). Also, this quantity of percentage is equal to what is later named (namely: "wheels as well as ironworks," etc.).

6. *the church of San Pedro and San Felices* is only one church—la iglesia de San Pedro y San Felices. This could be interpreted otherwise in English.

[Translation by Carlos Albaracin Sarmiento, Professor Emeritus of Spanish at the University of California at Santa Barbara, and Roberto de Souza, professor of Spanish at the University of La Plata, Argentina. Transcribed by Tommy Davison, University of California at Santa Barbara.]

Bibliography and Notes

BIBLIOGRAPHY

Avina, Rose. *Land Grants in California* (unpublished manuscript). University of California at Santa Barbara, Library.

Ayala, Pedro Lopez de. *Las Crónicas de Los Reyes de Castilla.* University of California at Santa Barbara, Library.

Bancroft, Hubert Howe. *History of California,* Volume 2. San Francisco: The History Company, 1886.

Benefield, Hattie. *For the Good of the Country . . . Por el Bien del País.* Los Angeles: Lorrin L. Morrison, Publisher, 1951.

Bolton, Herbert Eugene. *History of Duchess County, New York.*

Burke, Ulick Ralph. *History of Spain,* Volume 2. London: Longmans, Green & Co., 1895

Carrillo, Leo. *This California I Love.* Englewood Cliffs, N.J.: Prentice-Hall, 1961.

Dakin, Susanna Bryant. *A Scotch Paisano: Hugo Reid's Life in California, 1932-1852.* Berkeley: University of California Press, 1939.

Davis, William Heath. *Seventy-five Years in California.* San Francisco: John Howell Books, 1929.

Engelhardt, Rev. Zephyrin. *The Missions and Missionaries of California.* Volume I. San Francisco: The James H. Barry Co., 1908-1915.

Fernandez, Augustín Rodríguez. *Altamira Revista de Estudios Montaneses.* (Article in) Institución Culutral de Santander, 1972.

Hitchcock, Albert Spear. *Manual of the Grasses of the United States.* Washington, D.C.: U.S. Government Printing Office, 1935 (rev. 1950).

Hittell, Theodore H. *History of California.* Vol. 1. San Francisco: N.S. Stone & Co., 1897.

Hoffman, Ogden. *Hoffman's Land Cases.* San Francisco: Numa Hubert, Publisher, 1862. Reprinted by Yosemite Collections, 1975.

Hooton, [ ]. *Emigrants to America.* Folder F, Volume 2, p. 285. Public Record Office (Chancery Lane), London.

Keller, Werner. *The Bible As History.* New York: William Morrow & Co., 1952.

Ogden, Adele. *The California Sea Otter Trade, 1784-1848.* Berkeley and Los Angeles: University of California Press, 1941.

Ord, Angustias de la Guerra. *Occurrences in Hispanic California.* Washington, D.C.: Academy of American Franciscan History, 1956.

Prago, Albert. *The Revolutions in Spanish America.* New York: Macmillan, 1970

Robinson, Alfred. *Life in California.* New York: Wiley and Putnam, 1846.

Russell, Joseph H. *Cattle on the Conejo.* Los Angeles: Ward Ritchie Press, 1957.

Salmón, Mateo Escagedo. *Solares Montaneses.* Torrelavega, Spain: "Artes Graficas (Fernandez)," 1933.

Sands, Frank. *A Pastoral Prince.* (self-published), 1893.

Strain, Ethel H., and Hollister, Kathryn K. *The Ancestors and Descendants of Albert G. Hollister.* Santa Barbara, Calif.: W.T. Genns, Publisher, 1970.

Thompson, Rev. Joseph. *El Gran Capitan.* Los Angeles: Cabrera & Sons, 1961.

Tompkins, Walker A. *King of the Sheep Barons: The Life and Times of Colonel W.W. Hollister* (unpublished manuscript), Santa Barbara Historical Society, 1960.

Schurz, William Lytle. *The Manila Galleon.* New York: E.P. Dutton & Co., 1939.

SOURCES

Archivos de Santander; Santander, Spain

Congressional Globe. University of California at Santa Barbara, Library.

De la Guerra Archives, Santa Barbara Mission Archive Library.

Dibblee, Albert. Letters. Baker Library, University of California/Berkeley, Bancroft Library.

Encyclopaedia Britannica. Eleventh edition.

Great Register. Principal probate registry. Somerset House, London.

Halls of Records: Los Angeles County Courthouse, Santa Barbara County Courthouse.

Huntington Museum, Pasadena.

Poett. Family letters. Santa Barbara Historical Society.

NOTES

THE DE LA GUERRAS:

1. Fernandez, p 62; Salmón, v. 6, p. 17-18.
2. Burke.
3. Tessier. *A complete treatise on merinos.* 1811, translated from the French. p. 1.
4. Sutherland, C.H.V. *Gold, its beauty, power, and allure.* (rev. ed.) pp. 87-90.

5. Salmón.

6. Encyclopaedia Britannica, v. 16, p. 453 et seq.

7. Fernandez.

8. Juan de la Guerra. *Will and testament.* October 21, 1623 (addenda).

9. Encyclopaedia Britannica, v. 19, p. 160.

10. De la Guerra. *Will and testament.*

11. Fernandez, p. 71.

12. Thompson, p. 4.

13. ibid, p. 17.

14. Fernandez, p. 76.

15. ibid, p. 63.

16. Thompson, p. 2.

17. ibid, p.5.

18. ibid.

19. De la Guerra archives.

20. Thompson, p. 4.

21. De la Guerra archives.

22. Thompson, p. 16.

23. ibid, p. 17.

24. Prago, p. 73.

25. Map of Mexico.

26. De la Guerra archives.

27. ibid

28. Thompson, p. 18

29. Hittell, v. 1, p. 81.

30. Keller, p. 74, 143.

31. Tompkins, p. 76.

32. Benefield.

33. Davis.

34. ibid

35. Avina.

36. Davis.

37. Avina.

38. Hoffman.

39. Ord, p. 45.

40. Hoffman, p. 27

41. De la Guerra family documents, Santa Barbara Historical Society.

42. Thompson, p. 87.

43. Bolton.

44. Thompson, p. 6.

45. Ogden.

46. De la Guerra archives, folder 444, p. 298.
47. Hittell, v. 1, p. 526.
48. ibid
49. ibid, p. 527.
50. Dakin, p. 115.
51. Hittell
52. Daken
53. Santa Barbara Mission Archives Library
54. ibid
55. ibid
56. De la Guerra Archives
57. Santa Barbara Mission Archives Library
58. Hoffman
59. Russell
60. Hoffman
61. ibid
62. ibid
63. Carrillo
64. Tompkins
65. Thompson

THE DIBBLEES AND HOLLISTERS:
  1. Strain
  2. Tompkins
  3. ibid
  4. Boton
  5. Dibblee letters
  6. Hittell
  7. Dibblee letters
  8. ibid
  9. Tompkins
10. ibid
11. ibid
12. ibid
13. ibid
14. Dibblee letters
15. ibid
16. Dibblee-Poett letters
17. Dibblee letters
18. ibid
19. ibid

20. ibid
21. ibid
22. ibid
23. A. Dibblee Poett letters
24. Dibblee letters
25. ibid
26. Tompkins
27. ibid

The de la Guerra Family

JOSÉ ANTONIO JULIAN DE LA GUERRA (m. Maria Antonia Juliana Carrillo)

RITA de JESÚS*	RAIMUNDO*	JUAN JOSÉ*	LEÓN*	GASPAR*	JOAQUIN*	ANTONIO MARIA*

JOSÉ ANTONIO	MARIA TERESA	MARIA de las ANGUSTIAS	FRANCISCO ANTONIO
(m. Concepción Ortega)	(m. Wm. E.P. Hartnell)	(m. Manuel Jimeno)	(m. Asunción Sepulvida)
José Antonio	Guillermo	Manuela	Francisco
José Ramon	Juan	Maria Antonia	Maria Antonia
Guillermo	Adelberto	Angustias	
Alejandro	Uldarcio	Carolina	(m. Concepción Sepulveda)
Dolores	Pablo	José Antonio	Juan
Catarina	José	Porfírio	Osvaldo
Solá	Benamino	Santiago	José
Christina	Natimiles	Enrique	Hercules
Juana	George	Belisario	Pablo
	Franco	Juan	Anival
	Teresa		Anita
	Matilda	(m. Dr. James Ord)	Erlinda
	Madelina	Rebecca	Rosa
	Amelia		Diana
	Manuela		
	Anita		

PABLO ANDRES	ANNA MARIA	MIGUEL	MARIA ANTONIA
(m. Josefa Moreno y Castro)	(m. Alfred Robinson)	(m. Trinidad Ortega)	(m. Cesario Lataillade)
	James	Olympia	Carlos
	Elena	Maria	Maria Antonia
	James Miguel	Josefa	Cesario
	Anita	Joaquina	
	James II	Paulina	(m. Gaspar Oreña)
	Alfred	Carolina	Leopoldo
			Dario
			Anita
			Orestes
			Serna
			Arturo
			Acacia

PABLO ANDRES (m. Josefa Moreno y Castro)

CARLOS*	FRANCISCA	HERMINIA	DELFINA*
	(m. Thomas Dibblee)	(m. Charles Lee)	

TERESA*	FRANCISCA	YNEZ*	MERCEDES	WILSON	CARMELITA	WILLIAM*	DELFINA*
	(m. Wm. T. Summers) Dibblee Frances		(m. Alfred R. Poett)	(m. Anita Oreña)	(m. Francis T. Underhill)		

		THOMAS	VIRGINIA	YVONNE	RICHARD

FREDERICA*	YNEZ NANICE MERCEDES	ALFRED DIBBLEE*	HAROLD HOWARD
	(m. C.E. Russell)		(m. Mary Louise Hart)

CAROLINE	DELFINA	JOSEPH	JAMES	SUSAN	WILLIAM

Unmarried